Time

And Other Fragile Gifts

Time

And Other Fragile Gifts

Memoirs

By Mary Ellen Tomaszewski

Print information available on the last page.

Rev. date: 02/20/2015

Editor: Jennifer Linney
Cover Painting: Sue Pisarra Krisher
Cover Design Layout, Author Photo, and photo By the Garden: Nancy Ann Bowe
Reader: Elizabeth Roberts Daly

The prayer-poem, "Non-judgment" is excerpted from *Prayers to Sophia* by Joyce Rupp, ©2004. Used by permission of the publisher, Sorin Books®, an imprint of Ave Maria Press®, Inc., P.O. Box 428, Notre Dame, Indiana, 46556, www.avemariapress.com.

To order additional copies of this book, contact:
Xlibris
1-888-795-4274
www.Xlibris.com
Orders@Xlibris.com
657080

CONTENTS

Foreword 9

Acknowledgments 11

Introduction 15

Grandmother Remembers . . . Maybe 17

City Lessons 23

It's Different 27

Last Stop, Brooklyn 32

Morning Glory 39

Playgroup 45

Mandalas 50

September 56

Close Enough 60

Valentine's Day Times 12 65

The Way They Were 69

The Perpetual Piano Student 76

Careful With That Glass, Things Can Break 82

From One Mouth to Another Ear 88

Where's Dad? 94

Dance 104

Campaign 2008 111

Christmas: A Little This, A Little That 113

Gutsy Little Gracie 120

Worth and Dignity, Homemade 124

Lizzy 128

If the Bracelet Fits 139

A Poopsie 143

Who Owns What? 149

A letter to Madeline Dunham—Barack Obama's Grandmother 153

Getting and Giving the Best 156

My High School Graduation 161
Whistles and Other Warnings 163
Today, This Night, Right Now 168
Blessed are the Flexible 172
On Becoming Bop 180
Watch Out, Listen Up, and Be Grateful 182

Dedicated

To my mother, Anne Reichert,

&

To my husband, Tom, and our family

Foreword

We are each born into given and chosen legacies from our families: what we choose to pass down to our children, what we try to tuck away, what they discover on their own by way of imitation, mimicry, or insistence into our heart of hearts. I imagine early parents became storytellers to stave off the vulnerability of rearing children. We tweak or enlarge, look closer or veil, in order to prepare and protect them from the journey they are sure to have. In doing so, we often forget how we, too, are the characters they learn from.

This is the legacy I was born into—given and chosen. I was born into a family of storytellers, with my mother at the helm. These chronicles—her friendships, loves, heartbreak, and continued curiosity along the way—were often my teachers. They are so colorful in detail and recounting, I am often baffled that they are not my own memories, my own formative years, my own close friends. As you, too, will discover, there were times of dark, silent sadness and times made only for raucous laughter.

As her daughter, I leave you with this: The audacity of a writer that differs from a storyteller—that bold stretch that this book allows and that you, reader, make possible—is the invitation of others. Authors do not get to leave the room on a high note, do not get to pour more wine so one forgives or forgets easily. The printed page is always there in the morning. Instead, authors make offerings to the world and prayerfully let go.

A storyteller's life—my mother's life—is one made by paying attention and searching for someone with whom it could be shared. To you, she entrusts her experience, her truths, her careful remembering.

Kim Wildszewski

Rev. Kimberly Wildszewski, Parish Minister
Unitarian Universalist Church at Washington Crossing
Titusville, N.J

Acknowledgments

My first note of gratitude goes to Sara Bloom, instructor of the Memoir-Writing Workshop that I've attended for several years. Sara leads the class by administering doses of firmness, gentleness, and encouragement in just the right amounts. For all that you share, and for the generosity of your time, my heartfelt thank you, Sara.

Thank you, fellow class writers. Your stories have inspired me, and your kind hearts have enabled me to trust while sharing mine.

To my fellow congregants at the North Fork Unitarian-Universalist Fellowship: I've appreciated your laughs, sighs, and groans—all expressed in the appropriate places— while you listened to some of these essays.

When my husband, Tom, was growing up, he had a lot of bedtime stories read to him. Then, he grew up and did plenty of his own bedtime reading. Then, I started writing. In addition to being an avid reader, he became a devoted listener. Thank you, Tom.

Our kids, Zac, Jeremy, and Kim, have read a couple of these essays and their spouses, Michelle, Jess, and Tara have, as well. Michelle read the essay, "Lizzy." A day earlier, she'd bought a pretty hand towel for her and Zac's new home imprinted with the words "Simplify. Live Well. Laugh Often. Love Much." After reading about my sister Liz, Michelle was moved to gift me with her new purchase, a small item with a generous thought.

When I was feeling stuck while trying to write the introduction, I aired my frustrations to my daughter Kim. We agreed I'd send her what I wrote and, in the meantime, she'd write an introduction that I might use. In the end, I kept my introduction and have used Kim's as a foreword. I've heard forewords are often written by people of esteem. That seemed like a perfect match to me. Thanks, Kim.

You have all warmed my heart by encouraging me in different ways. Thank you.

To my grandchildren, Madison, Shawn, Leah, and those yet to come: You have inspired me to record reflections on my life and pass them down. As you grow—and as I continue to get to know you—I ponder that perhaps one day this collection will be a way of you knowing me. That is, knowing me more than as the grandmother you call "Bop," knowing a bit of the girl I was in what will be, for you, "the olden days."

I've been fortunate to have the gift of enduring friendships. Some of you are mentioned just a single time in these essays, some not at all. With you, I shopped for my first bra, survived Catholic school, talked out my fears, challenged my beliefs, shared holidays, took road trips, walked, and prayed. You still make me laugh until I cry, and, when I cry, you stick around until I can laugh again. You are women with integrity and faith. You have taught me, by your example, deep compassion. You've given me the greatest laughs and the best books.

Knowing you were there—dependable and loving—I could change and still have your trust and acceptance. I could bear my mistakes. I could grow. You are cherished new friends who never felt new, because you're so much like my treasured old friends. You were enablers while I was becoming more and more authentically me, more and more capable of knowing myself and being truthful. Thank you.

I have five brothers and three sisters. To Albie and Liz, whose passing was way too soon: Thank you for the times I have felt your presence.

To John, Anne, Bob, Bill, Patty, and Michael: Before joining a memoir writing class, I jotted down my thoughts in a black- and-white notebook. I would use early morning or late night to squeeze in journaling time. But one day, thoughts just wouldn't settle down and wait. I went to my computer and wrote in the middle of the day. The end result was the essay "Last Stop, Brooklyn." You knew some of the people I wrote about so, timidly, I sent it to you. Your responses encouraged me. Soon, I no longer waited for a certain time of the day to write. I rearranged my priorities, changing my writing time to Almost Any Time.

Where I have written about our family, my memories and perspectives may differ from yours. I didn't dare ask for much input. It's reasonable to expect I'd get a variety of valid accounts of any one incident that we all experienced. My favorite example of that reality is the fable "Five Blind Men," which David Roth turned into a song. It ends with these words:

For they had blessed me with a gift, a sparkling truth revealed

Whatever you might think you see
Depends on where you stand
And how you feel.

For those rare times when I asked, I'm grateful for what you offered. Thank you, Michael, for gifting each of us with a copy of our father's journal. From it, I gained valuable insight that enabled me to write about a man I barely knew.

To Tom's sister, Kathy: Thank you for the support you always so readily and lovingly give.

Nancy Ann Bowe, author of *The Honey Bee Portrait*, a book of macro photography and information on our true best friends and precious pollinators: Thank you for your graphic-design expertise on the layout and lettering for this book cover, as well as the back cover photo.

Jennifer Linney, editor, long-distance hand-holder: I have appreciated your clever humor as much as your editing skills. I've been reminded often how seizing time can be challenging. Sometimes my skimpy bit of writing time was reminiscent of my mother's way of divvying up dessert when there wasn't quite enough to go around: She would have us draw straws to see who would win a sliver of cake. When it came to writing time, for one good reason or another, I often just couldn't draw the long straw. My feelings of frustration have been expressed perfectly by the witty and unique Dr. Seuss:

How did it get so late so soon?
It's night before it's afternoon.
December is here before it's June.
My goodness how the time has flewn.
How did it get so late so soon?

I have appreciated your patience, Jennifer. It's been slow moving and often tedious, but you've kept it fun. Finally, what I am most grateful for is this: When I wanted to quit this project, you wouldn't let me. Thank you.

The Cover Artist: Sue Pisarra Krisher. When it came to the cover art, my hopes were high that my dear life-long friend Sue Pisarra Krisher would agree to do it. Sue was an art major when we were college roommates. When she wasn't pleased with a piece she was working on, she'd toss it in our dorm room wastebasket. In awe of her talent, I'd retrieve the discarded art, keeping it as a treasure.

Our friendship took us through the changes of young adulthood as we navigated the tumultuous mid-1960s. In the early '80s, to honor my birthday, Sue wrote about our friendship in a piece that was published in a New England regional paper called *Seacoast Women*. She wrote about us keeping in touch with "overwritten letters that make the envelopes bulge." Sue wrote the piece after visiting our home on Long Island. Our family was growing—our first son, a toddler; the second, a baby. Disposable diapers were available, but I hadn't yet given in to the use of them. Activism I felt inclined to express was sometimes limited to expressions on tee shirts.

In Sue's essay, "White Page," she wrote, in part:

> *All the props and the characters were there . . . children, pets, toys, homemade cookies . . . and the needlepoint pillow that supported my back as we talked through the 11 o'clock feeding. [Mary Ellen] . . . sat there in her T-shirt that read, "A woman's place is in the house . . . and in the senate" as she folded huge towers of diapers. We laughed about this and about many things. . . . I could see that the laugh wrinkles radiating from her eyes had deepened, and . . . I felt grateful to have helped to make them. . . . As we waved goodbye that day, I found myself yearning to be very old friends. . . . The ageless being in me is teaching me that the past and the future are written in disappearing ink. It is only right now that real life is happening. It is this moment that is the clean, white page . . . this moment.*

The gift of Sue's friendship is reflected in several essays. Thank you, Sue, for the joy of seeing my simple essays wrapped with your amazing art.

Introduction

If I were to grade My Past Self on how well I did being authentically me, I'd give myself barely a passing grade. So I didn't like looking back. That thought slipped my mind when I signed up for a class in memoir writing.

As an adult, I had used writing to clarify feelings or to savor a memory. For class, I write with some structure. I learned that unlike biographies, that tell the story of a lifetime, memoirs are snapshots of the past - memories that we bring into focus to examine details, to reflect on.

The energy of my writing group, under the leadership and guidance of Sara Bloom, has a subtle, but strong, affect on me. Group energy is like that. Musicians, meditation groups, painting classes - generally there's some good shared energy. During the months the class meets, I know I'll write, because stuff comes up, and I'll need to write.

I never intended to share my writing outside of class. But the more I wrote, the more I became interested in having the essays neatly bundled together in a collection. Maybe it's akin to what a parent might feel when all the kids, grown and getting along, are together for even just a night, under one roof.

My essay topics include activism, spirituality, family, and growing older, to name a few. I write about being born into my grandfather's crowded household in Queens, New York, and events from my childhood after we moved to a small town on eastern Long Island. For the most part, I resisted writing my version of the Catholic school craziness in favor of remembering the nuns who enriched my life, and the friends whose kindness and humor saved me from despair.

My editor, Jennifer Linney, writes the popular blog "Bug and the Sweet Banana." In a memorable post called *Love and All That Good Stuff*, Jennifer wrote a simple sentence when she explained her reason for blogging. It stayed with me: "The thing is, the bad stuff is easy to remember, and it's the good stuff that I don't want to forget."

I became a blogger after my first grandchild was born. It was a practical way for me to share with my family my days with our granddaughter. Jennifer helped me turn a year of blog posts into a treasured book called *Time with Madison*. I think Madison is exceptional in many ways. But she's also a normal child. So at times, she tried my patience, had tantrums, needed a timeout, and so forth. The book contains none of those times. It's our sweet memories—our laughs, her innocence, my joy—that's documented in the cherished stories.

That's not to say writing keeps the negative away or that it should. Sometimes, I feel my mind is a vessel whose job it is to collect negative thoughts. Like dealing with invasive weeds in the garden, I need to keep watching the thoughts I let in, to reserve space for the gift of now—the present time. Humorist Art Buchwald said, "Whether it's the best of times or the worst of times, it's the only time we've got."

I've left dates on the essays, indicating when they were written. In some cases, if I wrote on the same subjects today, the essays would be different – maybe a different tone, different characters added, different feelings. That's what time does. I've learned from my husband Tom that even the atoms that once made up my body are different atoms today. Physics aside, (now there's a phrase I've never used before) one who met and knew me decades ago might accurately say: We've met. I know who she is. What can't be said is: I know her. No matter how you measure the past – in decades, years, months or even days, we change. Most of us for the better.

I was in my 20s when I owned a book called *Be Here Now* by Ram Dass. I owned the book for quite a while before I opened it. It sat on my bookshelf made of concrete blocks and wooden planks, its title in full view, where I could see it. I'm still working on living the message of those few words.

Recently, I discovered the moonflower plant. When the light fades, the moonflowers begin to open. I had never heard of such a plant. Why, I wondered, would a gardener bother with a plant that blooms when few would see it? But the more I learned the more I felt grateful for nature's gift of this unusual flower. Its presence reminds me that dark times, too, can yield gifts. It was revealing to me to find I was in sync with nature like I hadn't felt before. Blossoming. When no one was looking.

"If you have a garden and a library, you have everything you need."
—*Cicero, Roman scholar and politician, 103-43 B.C.*

Grandmother Remembers . . . Maybe

I winced when Tom suggested a Chevy Impala for our next new car.

"It's not your mother's Impala," he said, calmly defending his suggestion.

I actually have fond memories of my mother's cars. She took excellent care of them, paying attention to any little ping that sounded out of the ordinary. And most significantly, it was on whatever car my mother owned that my siblings and I all learned to drive.

My mother was a no-nonsense kind of parent, and when she took us out for driving lessons, we paid close attention. "Pull up next to that parked car," she would say. "Back up until your front door lines up with its back door. Turn the wheel as you back in." Moving a little forward, a little back, it was done—and just the right distance from the curb.

I often get to practice my mother's lessons when I'm near home on Love Lane in Mattituck. Sometimes it's as though she's still sitting next to me. I feel a sense of pride when I parallel park well on the first try.

The cars that my mother had as I was growing up had manual transmissions with stick shifts on the steering column. That meant you had to manually change gears. My mother explained it this way: "Imagine the letter H. Neutral is where the short line connects the two longer ones. For first gear, you pull the gear shift toward you and down.

"As you increase speed, you need second gear. That's on the upper part of the H, but away from you. Straight down from second you have third gear. Reverse is above first gear."

Of course, there's more to shifting gears than moving a stick. Shifting has to coordinate with a third pedal called the clutch. Before shifting, your left foot has to apply just the right amount of pressure on the clutch at just the right time.

The Impala that I drive now—I came around to Tom's way of thinking—is much simpler. It's smaller, and it's an automatic. No clutch pedal. No stick shift. Small and simple.

For Christmas 1989, I thought I had given my mother a simple but interesting gift: a book called *Grandmother Remembers: A Written Heirloom for My Grandchild.* My mother was 71 at the time. She developed Alzheimer's disease in her mid-80s. Before that, she had a heart condition but a perfectly fine memory.

I imagined that her 20 grandchildren and 20-plus great-grandchildren would all benefit from the memories she would share in the book. But at the back of the book, my mother wrote a note, apologizing for not answering many of the questions. "I wanted this to be a happy book," she wrote, "so we'll skip the things that are sad." I didn't think any of the questions probed into "things that are sad," but that was my perspective.

Throughout her life, my mother dealt with abandonment, powerlessness, and loss, some of which was not unlike many women of her generation. In 1918, when my mother was born, her mother was just 16 years old and unmarried. She gave her infant daughter to an older married sister who was childless. As far as I know, there isn't a record of a legal adoption. It was a family matter.

Perhaps, the questions in the grandmother book just didn't seem relevant to my mother's life. Some people spend years hoping for the day that they'll hear they will be grandparents. My mother didn't have that mindset, that luxury of anticipating the birth of the next generation. As a nine-year-old, I remember being extremely excited about the news that my oldest brother, Al, and his wife were having a baby. My six other siblings and I would all be aunts and uncles. My parents would be grandparents.

When the baby was born my mother was 39, now a new grandmother, and also pregnant with her ninth child. Just 10 days before she gave birth to our new brother, a tugboat accident took the lives of Al and my father. Al's wife, Eileen, and baby girl, Mary Anne, moved in with our family for almost two years. During that horrendously difficult time, our home and our family life was blessed with, not one, but two beautiful babies.

In my mother's *Grandmother Remembers* book, there's a section called "Thoughts I'd Like to Share with You" with a sentence awaiting completion: "I'm proud of _____." My mother left it blank.

I wish I had sat with her and that we had worked together on the book. I wouldn't have allowed her to leave that sentence blank. I would have reminded her about her activism for positive change. I would not have let her put down the pen until she had written about what she did to help our community. I would have prodded her to write: "I organized a committee to plan the first library in our town."

I remember the day my mother came home from the library in nearby Center Moriches. She talked with a mix of anger and disappointment, like one would talk about a nagging annoyance: "Why don't we have a library? Every other town has a library." Because of the reckless way that our town was built, it ended up looking beat up and lacking such basic luxuries as a library. My mother got the ball rolling for the construction of a library, which wound up being a vibrant place in the community.

The grandmother book also asked about family traditions, family recipes, and dear relatives. We had all of those, but perhaps they didn't look the way my mother imagined they should. Those sections are among the pages that she had left blank.

If she used 1950s TV programs as her frame of reference for the typical family, then I can understand the blank pages. Our family life wasn't reflected in those TV shows, not by a long shot.

I suppose my mother wasn't able to see that she had singlehandedly created our family's traditions: We ate home-cooked dinners together every night. We attended church together every Sunday. We shared big Thanksgiving dinners. We hung homemade stockings at Christmastime. My younger sisters and I dressed for Easter in matching dresses that our mother had made.

My mother didn't have siblings, and she had a step-mother who wasn't at all a homemaker, so I can see that she'd get stuck on the page entitled, "Family Recipes." But today, her kids and grandkids make many of the meals that she had made for her large family. Some of the favorites are her delicious beef stew and her chicken soup. Her tasty bread pudding was a good way to make use of leftover bread, and it doubled as a snack or a dessert.

Had my mother been asked, "What did you teach your kids about food?" she could have written paragraphs. I'm certain she would have written, "Pay attention to good nutrition. Sit down together as a family. When possible, say yes when your kids want a friend to stay for dinner." She was so good about that.

I sort of understand my mother's reluctance to look back in order to fill in the pages of that grandmother book. When I first signed up at the Southold Town Recreation Center for a memoir-writing workshop, I somehow overlooked the word "memoir." I paid the workshop-registration fee, and only later did it dawn on me: I'd be writing about the past.

Generally speaking, I'm not fond of going there. But I like writing, I like people, and I like the energy of a group, so, in spite of having what we all have—memories and regrets that can be painful—I'm accepting the challenge of remembering and writing. In fact, I quickly sign up any time the workshop is offered.

It's my turn now to fill in the blanks on the pages of a grandmother book. My book is more inclusive: It's called *A Grandparent's Book*. It's for Grandma *and* Grandpa. In our case, we would say "Babcia" and "Dziadzie," as Tom and I decided to use the Polish words for "Grandma" and "Grandpa" to keep that connection with his proud Polish heritage. Our titles have taken a personal touch, though: We're just simply "Bop" and "Joj."

My Chevy Impala is not my mother's oversized Impala with the manual transmission, and the grandparent book that I received last Christmas isn't the book that I gave my mother. My car is smaller and simpler, but my book is neither.

The older book is about 50 pages long. Mine is 143 pages. The questions are so much more—should I say—contemporary: "Did you marry more than once?" Unless we opt to skip that question, just as my mother skipped so many, I would answer no. Tom would answer yes. That question is followed by "Whom?" And although I have never had any adverse feelings toward Tom's high-school girlfriend, whom he married while in college, I'm not sure about adding her name to our special grandparent's book. It feels a bit odd and unnecessary.

The book also probes, "Have you ever gone to a psychiatrist or a psychologist?" and "What do you think about therapy?"

There are 16 categories of questions in our grandparent book. They're about growing up, travel, work, money, family lore, religion, traditions, hobbies, history, and politics to name just some of them. I will be doing memoir writing for the rest of my life.

Now that we have Madison, our six-month-old granddaughter, our grandparent book has taken on new meaning. We have a real audience in mind, especially for our response to a question way in the back of the book: "What do you hope the future holds for me?" So as not to be trite, that answer requires some serious thought.

Less serious is my wondering about the kind of car our granddaughter will drive. I wonder, if she hears the words "Chevy Impala," will she even recognize them as words that identify a kind of car? Tom drives a '97 Pontiac Grand Prix made by General Motors, the same company that makes Chevys. His Pontiac has over 196,000 miles on it, and he's still enjoying the ride. But GM is struggling to survive, and it has stopped making Pontiacs.

Still, we'll have our pictures. Seeing photos with cars in them is like catching a glimpse of a fond old friend in the background: They're noticed, and they so often invite reminiscing.

Maybe there will be an Impala or some other GM car in Madison's future, maybe not. But I know I'd better get busy remembering and filling in some answers to questions.

The author of my grandparent book says it's "an adventure in nostalgia." It may also be an adventure that has me driving my little Impala to memoir-writing workshops for many years to come.

Fall 2009

Update: In February 2013, Tom traded in his Pontiac with 226,000 miles on it and is now the proud owner of a 2012 GMC pickup.

Mastics-Moriches-Shirley Community Library

25th
Anniversary Ceremony

*In recognition of
the original founders
of the Community Library*

Sunday, October 3, 1999

Greetings and Introductions .... *William Cicola*
Director

Star Spangled Banner .... *Aiofe Browning*

Welcome .... *Barbara Keenan*
President, Board of Trustees

Audio Visual Retrospective

Recognitions:
  Original Library Committee & Former Trustees .... *J. Robert Verbesey*
  Founding Director

  Staff .... *William Cicola*
  Director

Library Beginnings
  Grassroots Efforts to Establish a Library .... *Ann Reichert*
  Chairperson of Ad Hoc Committee

The Library's Early Years .... *Ray Supino*
  Elected Member of First Board of Trustees

Closing Words .... *William Cicola*
  Director

Benediction .... *Reverend Joseph Mirro*

Thanks to people like my mother, the community where I was raised has a library.

"Sometimes I lie awake at night, and I ask, 'Where have I gone wrong?'
Then a voice says to me, 'This is going to take more than one night.'"
—*Charles M. Shulz*

City Lessons

I saw a small group of people gathered by the post office in Laurel, Long Island, near where I live. A few people who seemed to know each other stood talking. One person sat nearby on a bench that marks this space as "The Bus Stop." The bus this group would catch any minute now is called "The Hampton Jitney." It runs from the east end of Long Island to New York City and is a pretty decent ride.

Each passenger is allowed only one call on a cell phone for only a whispered minute, a call that a passenger might use to say, "We're on time. Whose car should I look for?" Each passenger gets a muffin, a drink, and a comfortable seat.

I became familiar with this method of traveling when our daughter, Kim, used it frequently while studying as a seminary student in Manhattan. I wondered what the people at the bus stop on this day would do when they got to the city, and I remembered a few of my times there.

When I was a freshman college student, everything was frighteningly new to me. It was a blessing that on Day One, I met Sue, who would be my roommate and my dear, close friend for life. One day while on break during that first year, Sue and I made plans to visit another college friend who lived in New Jersey. I was nervous about the weekend. I had never been to our friend's home before and hadn't yet met her family. Sue convinced me it would be fun—something she often did over the years. When I think back, I'm surprised at the size of the suitcases we used for our two-night stay. We each had one that, today, I'd use for a two-week vacation, not for a weekend at a friend's home.

We took the train from Sue's hometown of Huntington into Manhattan. Wherever we were headed, we needed to go through a revolving door. I had minimal experience with the city, but I'm sure

I must have walked through revolving doors before. Well, the door turned, as revolving doors do, and Sue moved into the opening. I thought, in the interest of time or space, I should follow right behind her—not in the next section of the door, but with her, in the same little opening.

I've learned that's called "tailgating." That would have been OK, I guess, except one of our suitcases got stuck, keeping the door from moving. Sue and I pushed the door and tugged at the suitcase, but neither would budge. We pushed in the other direction and tugged the suitcase some more. We kept pushing, tugging, pushing, tugging. Nothing worked.

We went from feeling puzzled to frantic. The frustrating situation turned even more stressful—as well as embarrassing—when we saw people outside the big glass door, waiting for it to move so they could use it. We were keeping them from their usual fast pace.

The onlookers stood expressionless as Sue and I continued anxiously pushing, pulling, and tugging. Our frenzy turned to nervous laughter, and then, we were out of control. We laughed so hard we couldn't stand up. We crouched down, leaning on our suitcases for support, and both of us lost control of our bladders. Finally, someone on the other side of the door somehow freed the stuck suitcase. The doors turned, and Sue and I escaped from the revolving doors with whatever composure we could muster.

A year or so later, I visited the city alone. As I walked along the street, a name on a building caught my eye: Bankers Trust. "Oh, wow," I said to myself. Sue's father worked at Bankers Trust.

The father of my close friend, Maureen, worked in a bank, too. It was in Riverhead—her hometown—and where we both attended Catholic high school. Maureen's father was a custodian. Like Sue's father, he was a gentle man—hardworking and honest. He once found a lot of cash in a trash can. Maureen's father would have never considered doing anything but turning it in. The bank awarded him $50.

When I asked Sue what her father did at the bank, I was pretty sure she said, "He's vice-president."

I liked and felt comfortable with Sue's father, and when I saw Bankers Trust that day in Manhattan, I thought, "I might as well stop in and see Mr. Pisarra since I'm right here." I walked timidly to a teller and asked, "Is it possible to see the vice-president?"

She looked at me quizzically.

I immediately thought that I'd probably been presumptuous and added, "If he's not too busy with a meeting or lunch or something."

"You want to see the vice-president?" she asked.

"Yes," I said, politely. "He's my friend's father. I was just walking by and thought I'd stop in just to say hi, if that's OK."

"What's his name?" she asked.

I could understand a teller not knowing Maureen's father. He worked the night shift. But I knew for sure that Sue's father worked days. I found it curious that the teller didn't know him. She flipped through pages of typed papers stapled together. "We have a lot of vice-presidents," she explained.

I began to feel uncomfortable.

"If you give me a minute," the teller said, "I can tell you what branch he's in."

I wasn't experienced with the city, but I caught on. I thanked the teller just the same and left the bank. It was one of my many life lessons that came with a good degree of awkwardness.

I had a friend who used to see a psychic in Manhattan. She was certain I'd enjoy the experience, so I drove myself into the city, parked my car right outside the psychic's apartment, and did, indeed, find the session fascinating. When finished, I took the elevator down to the lobby and walked out onto the street. My mind was full of things I hadn't heard or thought of before. I think I walked with a bit of a smile on my face, still thinking about the intriguing session.

All of that changed rather drastically when I realized my car was gone. I read the parking sign that I thought I'd understood earlier. I was terrified once it became clear to me that my car had been towed.

I found a phone booth and made desperate calls to figure out what to do. I received directions to the garage where my car had been taken. I needed to take buses to reach it, buses that didn't have names but that were identified by colors and letters.

I couldn't comprehend the information. I might as well have been in a foreign country. I was alone and frightened.

Overwhelmed by the directions for buses and transfers, I decided on a slightly less tense option and took a taxi. Arriving at the garage, I saw gray, cold concrete everywhere and a woman who sat alone at a small table near the entrance. Her manner surpassed the coldness of all that concrete.

As I approached her, she kept her eyes on the papers in front of her. She asked me for my license plate number. I struggled, trying to remember it. Finally, I told her the number and then admitted I wasn't absolutely positive about the order of the last two numbers.

She said, "Ya can't get the car without the right plate number."

"Could you try looking up the one that I gave you? I think that might be it," I said with great trepidation.

"No," she said firmly, "One number. That's it. The right number."

Perhaps I could have left, searched for another phone booth, and called the psychic for help. But her expertise seemed to be with dead people. I'd had a great conversation with a couple of beloved relatives on The Other Side, oh, but I wish one of them would have noticed what was happening to my car on the street below. I did make a phone call—to my husband, who gave me the plate number. I got my car back, but I had to make a follow-up trip for an intimidating court appearance, where I paid a hefty fine for illegal parking.

I rarely use a revolving door without thinking of that day with Sue and the stuck suitcases. I don't know what I would have talked with her father about if I did happen upon the branch of the bank where he worked. Unlike the woman in the garage, Sue's father had a kind, easy manner. Conversation with him was always comfortable.

I wish I could say that driving by the people waiting for the bus in Laurel made me think of wonderful cultural experiences I'd had in New York City. But, to my dismay, I've spent too little time in the city. There's always been something holding me back—time, money, inexperience. I wasn't raised to think of the city as a source of wonder, stimulation, or entertainment. When my family moved from Queens to eastern Long Island in 1955, there was a sense of being saved from the monster. We were the lucky ones who were given the opportunity to live in the country.

Tom and I celebrated our 25th wedding anniversary with a trip to Italy. We went to Rome, Florence, and Venice. Our 35th anniversary is coming up, and it is probably a good time to do something different again. I think it would be exciting to see Prague or Barcelona, but maybe we'll just catch a bus and go into New York City.

June 2010

"I think, at a child's birth, if a mother could ask a fairy godmother
to endow it with the most useful gift, that gift would be curiosity."
—Eleanor Roosevelt

It's Different

For my 60th birthday celebration, I sent almost that number of invitations to women that I wanted to see in my home, to share a meal with, and mark time. I chose paper with a fall theme and put my thoughts in a lengthy rhyme. It read, in part,

I'm making some plans to celebrate . . . 60.
Yikes! It makes my heart palpitate.
I won't distress, and I mustn't get blue.
I'll get women together, that's what I'll do. . .
There're men in my life who are special to me.
But they'll sit this one out—it's women only.

I'm not sure why I wanted to surround myself with feminine energy as I entered my new decade. My mother and my younger sister, Liz, both died the year before, just months apart. Maybe, in some way that I don't quite understand, that had something to do with the make up of the party. Whatever the reason, it just felt right.

I have heard someone say that 60 is the new 40. I don't know if that's the case, but I do know that 60 got my attention in a way that other birthdays hadn't.

I was a little kid when my Aunt Marie started talking to me about aging. Every time I saw her, she'd make a fuss about my red hair and then she'd always add, "You'll be white by the time you're 40."

I was one of nine kids, but I was the only one she would say that to. I didn't know why, but I do know that, as a child, I didn't spend any time thinking about turning 40. And if I gave any thought at all to one day having white hair, I probably thought, "Well, when you're 40, you're old, and old people have white hair."

Of course, as I got older, 40-year-olds got younger. None of them that I knew had white hair, and I didn't either. Thanks to just the right mix of chemicals, I had managed to keep my hair red—the same pretty shade of red that I had as a kid.

The color came from my father's side of the family. My grandfather, Pop, and one of my uncles, the one that Aunt Marie was married to, were both redheads. I wore my hair in ponytails or braids, with and without bangs, in grade school. I wore it short and teased in high school and long and straight in college. I permed it when my kids were little and cut it real short later on.

Aunt Marie was Italian, sexy, and sometimes boisterous, in a fun way. She took great pleasure in repeating the story of, and her part in, the birth that took place in an upstairs bedroom at my grandfather's house.

Pop was a widower when my parents moved in with him for what was supposed to be a temporary arrangement. They had two young sons at the time—Albie, a toddler, and Johnny, an infant.

Most women in Queens, New York, delivered their babies in hospitals, and for her first five babies, my mother did, too. But my father was always at work and missed out on things like driving to the hospital, pacing the waiting room, and awaiting news of whether he had a son or a daughter and how mother and child were doing. Like his father, brother, and others in the family, he was a tugboat captain. Generally, he'd be on the boat a week, off a week, sometimes longer on than off. With her previous pregnancies, when my mother began serious labor in my father's absence, she'd arrange for child care and then ask Pop to take her to the hospital. If Pop wasn't available, she called a taxi.

My mother told me she thought that perhaps with a home birth, my father would get more involved. I'm not exactly sure what she meant by "get more involved."

My mother tried to be a faithful Catholic. The teachings of her church said, as they say today, that the rhythm method is the only acceptable method of birth control. My father was a non-practicing Lutheran. He enjoyed dancing and had a beautiful singing voice. But, from the stories that my mother told, that's as far as his interest in rhythm went. When he was home, my father really didn't care to hear about the monthly calculations that determined a good time or a bad time to be intimate with his wife. So, they had babies.

My mother's plans for a home birth included having a doctor present. Newspapers layered under the bed sheet protected the mattress. Aunt Marie was in the room to help and, in fact, administered the ether. What qualified her for that position, I think, was simply that she and my mother got along well. That was about it.

My father was on the boat. The rest of the family was downstairs, doing whatever they did on a Sunday evening. Albie was 11; Johnny, 9; Anne, 7; Bobby, 5; and Billy, 4. I asked my sister Anne what they were doing at the time and wondered if we had a TV. It was 1947. There were households with TVs in about a dozen big cities across the country, including New York.

Anne said, "We got the TV when Lizzy was born, either the day she was born or the day she came home from the hospital." That was in '49. Anne suggested she and our four brothers were probably listening to stories on the radio, stories like *The Lone Ranger*, *The Green Hornet*, *Fibber McGee and Molly*. She said, "We might have been reading comic books or playing a game. More likely, we were sitting on the edge of our seats with our eyes bugging out as we watched the doctor come in with his black bag and go to the bedroom upstairs where Mom was in labor and Aunt Marie was bustling around doing whatever was needed."

Those were the only details I'd ever heard, that and the part about right after the birth: Aunt Marie stood at the top of the stairs and—not caring if people in the next county could hear her—hollered to my sister and four brothers, "It's a girl! You have a sister! And she's a redhead!"

Anne told me, "I was only seven years old. It was all kind of mysterious to me, and a little scary, too, until I saw you, of course. That was amazing."

My mother said that her plan hadn't worked out exactly the way she had hoped. By the time my father got home from the boat, he walked into what was a pretty typical scene: Mom was at the stove, stirring oatmeal. "So? What did you have?" he asked.

My mother went back to having babies in the hospital. Three more were born after me, none of them redheads.

For years, I kept a standing appointment with my hairdresser—at first every four weeks, then closer to every three weeks as I tried to defy the white that Aunt Marie had predicted. Before celebrating 60, I colored my hair for the last time, although it wasn't planned like that. Like our big family, it just happened that way.

Going natural was something that I had wondered about enough to bring it up over lunch with a couple of childhood friends, Marilyn and Susan, both a couple of years older than me. Susan said that she, too, had thought about it occasionally. Marilyn said, "Never." I wasn't surprised. Her own mother, who is almost 90, still colors her hair. And yet it was Marilyn who gave me Anne Kreamer's book, *Going Gray*, as a birthday present. The subtitle reads, *What I Learned About Beauty, Sex, Work, Motherhood, Authenticity, and Everything Else That Matters*. It's that last phrase—authenticity, and everything else that really matters— that got my attention. An added influence were the pictures of women and their words in yet another birthday gift, a book by Joyce Tenneson called *Wise Women*.

I find myself looking in the mirror more often than I used to, and when I do, I see my older sister who was a brunette but is now light blonde. And I see my mother.

I find myself scrutinizing the appearance of the hard-to-find, white-haired women in magazines. And although I do appreciate compliments on my new look, I haven't solicited any opinions from anybody, with the exception of my husband. I think that asking others if they like my white hair would be akin to asking them if they like the way my eyes have gone from 20/20 vision to whatever my vision is today or asking them about the veins in my legs or my frown line. "Don't you like the way it draws attention from the smaller, less dramatic lines?" I imagine asking. My hair, eyes, legs, and face, they're all still doing some part of the job they were designed to do. They just don't look like they once did. They're different now.

Aunt Marie has passed on. I missed my chance to say, "Thanks for being there when Mom and I needed you. I'm sure Mom didn't have time for baby announcements, but from what I heard about your excitement and exuberance, there was no need for any other announcement. And thanks for the attention you gave a shy little redhead. I didn't see you much, but when I did, you sure made me feel special. You were right about turning white at 40, and I was wrong: Forty isn't old. Neither is 60. It's just different."

2008

A drive into Queens with Aunt Helen led us to stop by my late grandfather's house on 53rd Avenue in Elmhurst. The then-current owners graciously invited us to walk through my birthplace and old home.

"I like a teacher who gives you something to take home to think about besides homework."

—*Lily Tomlin*

Last Stop, Brooklyn

Ancient Mayan legend states that at the end of an evening, friends gathered around a bonfire and shared their hearts. They praised each other's qualities and reminisced on time that they had spent together. As the embers faded, the friendship was said to be sealed anew, the friends drawn closer together.

Many shops today sell circle-of-friends candleholders, terracotta pieces made in western Mexico that resemble a pre-Columbian art form. The candleholders consist of three to seven figures, standing or sitting in a circle, arms entwined. Although you can find a circle-of-friends candleholder in which the friends are frogs or basset hounds or snowmen, the crude figures most often resemble ancient Mayans. The idea is that the friends will never let go of each other's arms. Inextricably entwined, they symbolize the unbroken circle of friendship.

There were six of us who were close friends in high-school: Teri, Eileen, Liz, Maureen, Joe, and me. My circle-of-friends candleholder reflects our little social group.

My kids grew up hearing some of my Catholic high school horror stories, and they probably saw the card that I had in my home office that read, "I SURVIVED CATHOLIC SCHOOL." I guess my daughter absorbed the messages, because, years ago, Kim gave me a little plastic wind-up toy called "Nunzilla." Wind it up, and the nun appears to spit fire.

At Mercy High School in Riverhead in the early 1960s, I spent some time with more than one Nunzilla. They were the mean few who filled me with fear and anxiety.

But there was also light. The light was in the form of the nuns who were good people and outstanding teachers. The light was also in the friendships that I still treasure.

The terracotta candleholder and the plastic wind-up toy that spits fire are both symbols of those memorable years. The Nunzilla has been put away. I still light a candle in the piece that symbolizes the friendships.

When journalist Tim Russert died in June 2008, I watched and listened as his son and close friends paid tribute. Among the speakers was one of Russert's former teachers, a Catholic nun. I noticed that she spoke without once spitting fire. Rather, some would say, she was a Lightworker. She helped Tim Russert, the student, develop his innate talents and grow as a person. Her influence in his life was a source of nourishment.

The tribute made me think of Sister Lawrence, my junior- and senior-year English teacher. An intelligent, soft-spoken woman, she had high expectations of all her students. I loved her classes, although her serious demeanor kept me from relaxing in her presence. Years after we both left Mercy High School, I wrote to her. She wrote back as "Sister Marie Kennedy." Like many nuns, by this time, she had dropped the use of her religious name.

In the classroom, Sister Tomasina offered more of a balance. She taught business courses, and although she, too, took her coursework seriously, she let her easygoing, lightheartedness show. Her classroom had a relaxed atmosphere.

Before I entered Mercy High School, two of my older brothers, Bob and Bill, attended school there. After my father and oldest brother died, Sister Tomasina was one of the nuns who kept a close watch on my brothers. She stayed in touch with my mother many years afterward.

Like me, my younger sister, Liz, left Catholicism a few years after high school. Decades later, when Liz learned that she had bone cancer, she called Sister Tomasina from her home in Florida. They spoke often.

During that time, Sister Tomasina was diagnosed with a cancerous brain tumor. When I called to ask if I could visit with her at the Riverhead convent, she said, "Sure, as long as you understand that if I'm having a bad day, I'll have to cancel."

For one reason or another, a visit never happened. Too much time passed before I renewed my effort to see her. And when I did, I learned that she'd left Riverhead for care at the Sisters of Mercy Mother House in Brooklyn.

I felt deep regret that I had missed seeing her and wondered how I missed paying a respectful visit to someone who had lived only 10 minutes away. I've heard the words "the road to hell is paved with good intentions," and, although I didn't think I was headed for hell, I didn't like that I hadn't followed through on my good intentions.

Years ago, an acquaintance helped me to understand that it is never too late. Ginny told me that a whole year after her father had died she received a card expressing sympathy from someone who had just wanted her to know that she cared, despite the stretch of time that had passed. She said those thoughtful words meant a lot to her, even a year later.

I didn't know Sister Tomasina's family, so, in the event of her passing, there would be no one whom I would tell, "She was one of the good ones, and that was no small matter back then." So, I decided to go to Brooklyn. Teri, one of my high-school buddies who lived in East Hampton at the time, offered to join me.

It began snowing early on the morning of our journey to Brooklyn. On any other day, that would have been a good reason to reconsider the road trip. Never mind that I had never driven to Brooklyn before.

The drive was challenging. The first time we got lost, I at least understood why: The nun who had given me directions referred to "The Expressway," and I just assumed that she meant the Long Island Expressway. She meant the Brooklyn-Queens Expressway.

Even after Teri and I worked through that glitch, we still stumbled through the poor directions. The snow continued to fall. We grew hungry and frustrated. When we finally arrived at the Mother House, we received warm greetings, and, to our pleasant surprise, the sisters offered us lunch.

The nun who had greeted us walked us down an immense hallway with a ceiling that must have been about 30 feet high. The tiled floor and walls shone brilliantly. We stopped at elegant French doors that opened to a dining room and a scene that took us by surprise.

Inside, small groups of elderly women sat talking at 10 or so round tables. As the nun showed me and Teri to our table, the talk stopped. They watched us in silence.

"They're here to see Tomasina," the nun explained to our curious onlookers.

One of the women asked if we were Sister Tomasina's nieces.

"No, they're not her nieces," the nun replied. "They're former students from Riverhead."

Before Teri and I could sit, voices from the various tables peppered us with questions: "When were you in Riverhead?" "What are your names?" "Does Sister Tomasina know that you're here?" "How long are you staying?"

"I was in Riverhead," one of the nuns said. "I'm Sister Rosarita."

Teri and I were struck by how lonely some of the women seemed. They were so eager to talk and to have us listen. Rosarita, who had been our guidance counselor, shared with us that she was just 17 years old when she entered the convent, in her words, "a baby still." In her life outside of the Order, she had never interviewed or been hired for a job. She was working on an assignment that she enjoyed when she received a letter saying that she was to go to Riverhead to serve as the guidance counselor at the new high school there.

Sister Rosarita laughed and told us, "A guidance counselor, and I'd never held a job in my life." She told us about a Mercy High School graduate who returned to the school to visit. "I guess I didn't do a very good job," Sister Rosarita said. "He point-blank told me, 'You were my guidance counselor, and my life's been a mess.'"

Sister Rosarita mentioned another man who was pretty successful. Each time he visited, he reminded her that she had told him no college would accept his application for admission. She had been terribly grim about his future and told him so. "I guess he was glad to prove me wrong," she said, seemingly not taking life, or herself, very seriously.

When a nun at the table behind Teri and me heard us say that we had graduated from Mercy in 1965, she lost interest. "I was gone by then," she explained.

I mentioned my older brothers, and she remembered them. She recalled my brother Bob's "bushy black hair" and that "there were about seven other kids in the family." Not bad, considering that Bob had traipsed in and out of her life so briefly over 40 years earlier.

Teri and I learned that Sister Bernarda—the art teacher and a favorite of many students—had left the convent and married a priest. The nuns said the wedding was great fun and full of priests and nuns.

For the next couple of hours, Sister Rosarita visited with us. She pointed out a nun at the other end of the dining room who wore a blue sweater and a faraway look. "Do you remember Sister James?" Sister Rosarita asked. "She has Alzheimer's now and isn't doing well."

Sister James! One of the Nunzillas. Dreadfully mean.

Teri thought Sister James showed a flicker of awareness when she saw us and suggested we say hello. I followed behind reluctantly. Sister James managed to return our greeting, nothing more.

As we left the dining room, the nuns thanked us repeatedly for coming by. We were then off to another floor to visit Sister Tomasina.

The nuns in the dining room warned us more than once about how we would find her. One said she probably weighed 60 pounds. Another said 50 pounds.

Sister Tomasina was skeletal. I had to look at her from the doorway at first, and then gradually drew closer. It wasn't long at all before it felt good to see her. Sister Tomasina's face stayed expressionless, but she held our hands while we talked. She wasn't just responsive, she made us laugh. The nurse's instinct in Teri knew just how to refresh Sister Tomasina, doing thoughtful things like wetting her lips with water.

I talked about a time when Sister Tomasina had lunch at my house with another kind nun, Sister Hugh, my mother, and my mother's close friend, Ceil Mensch. Without hesitation, Sister Tomasina said my mother's name: "Anne Reichert."

"She's in a nursing home," I told her.

Sister Tomasina wanted to know where. The fact that she could speak at all, respond to us, and ask questions truly baffled me, considering how she appeared. It was hard to believe any life at all could come from that body.

Teri talked about caring for her mother, her work as a nurse, and her love of horses. "Do you like horses?" she asked Sister Tomasina.

"Not particularly," she responded.

I thought to myself, "On an average day, I have a hard time getting the word 'particularly' out—and spoken clearly."

Teri said she had never seen anyone in that stage of death that alert. We talked about the good friendships we still have and mentioned Joe. I remembered seeing Sister Tomasina and a couple of the other nuns at his funeral mass in September 1999. I thought about Fran—Joe's mom—and was glad the nuns were there. I'd wondered then if perhaps when a son dies of AIDS, you needed the presence of others even more so, to help bless his life and dignify his cruel death.

We told Sister Tomasina that we remembered how she used to start every shorthand class dictating as she walked through the door. She drilled us on what were called "brief forms," symbols that represented a group of words that were written together as one.

"I still use brief forms at times when I'm journaling," I shared, "like the symbol for 'should have,'" which looks like a check mark followed by a curved line.

Teri added, "Or 'should have been,'" which is written with another curved line going in the other direction.

In her little whisper, Sister Tomasina added, "'I should have been,'" and we laughed, remembering how long you could make a phrase in shorthand without ever lifting the pen. And we laughed because it was clear that Sister Tomasina was with us.

We remembered times when she would gently reprimand the class, saying, "Boys and girls, your manners are showing, and good manners never show."

As we prepared to leave, Teri suggested that we pray together. Normally, I might have worried about remembering the words, but I had a bit of confidence because I'd been taking my mother to the First Friday rosary services at the nursing home. Teri said when her mother had gone through a recent surgery, she spent a lot of time in the hospital chapel, remembering and reciting prayers from her earlier years. So, we both managed to get through a Catholic prayer, indirectly, with the help of our mothers.

Teri thanked Sister Tomasina for being a good teacher and a good person during years that were the best of times and the worst of times.

I cried.

We said our goodbyes, and Sister Tomasina took our hands to her face and kissed them. "Give everyone my love," she said with a weak whisper. "Come again. Come again."

As we left, Sister Rosarita showed us the chapel, an exquisite space with huge stained-glass windows. Instead of traditional pews that face the front, the seating is circular, leaving an empty round space at the center of the chapel. Wooden chairs with straight tall backs were shined to a high gloss.

Its beauty aside, I couldn't picture one person I saw in the dining room sitting in those chairs. As though she could read my mind, Sister

Rosarita said, "There's no one here interested in sitting in *those* seats anymore."

She shared that the Sisters of Mercy were trying to figure out what to do with the convent in Riverhead. Only five nuns live in its 35 rooms. Flip those numbers, and you have an image of what sometimes can be the living conditions for some of our immigrants, where 35 people might share five rooms.

When we said our goodbyes to Sister Rosarita, she said, "Now it's left for you younger people to do the work of the church."

I said, "Well—" starting to explain that I was no longer Catholic. I figured Teri would follow and offer that she, too, was no longer Catholic. She would have likely left out the part that her life partner is a woman, which would have disqualified her from doing "the work of the church." But I was interrupted.

Maybe it didn't matter, but I also didn't want to leave feeling like a fraud.

I thought about those words: "the work of the church." When the Bush administration moved toward war in Iraq, the Pope spoke out against it. If promoting peace is the work of the church, then I can embrace that. And there are some in the Catholic Church—perhaps, exclusively women—who are helping many to become familiar with, and appreciate, the feminine image of God. Count me in on that, too.

Sister Tomasina was a good woman and a good teacher. I don't remember anything poisonous ever shooting from her mouth. During our visit with her in her frail state, she made us laugh. She remembered my mother's name without hesitation. And she kissed our hands.

Just four days after our visit, I received word that Sister Tomasina had died. Brooklyn wasn't just *her* last stop; in a way it was mine, too, my last chance to show a kind, dying woman that I cared.

It was a last chance, and, as such things usually go, it was also a privilege.

2009

*"Sunsets, like childhood, are viewed with wonder
not just because they are beautiful, but because they are fleeting."*
—*Richard Paul Evans,* The Gift

Morning Glory

For many years, at the start of spring, I always intend to begin my garden by planting seeds indoors. It always sounds like a good idea, and this year, I actually did it. Tom and I visited with our son Jeremy and his wife, Jess, in their home in Delaware. Jeremy showed me the starter seed kit he had bought. He was happy with it, so I bought the same one.

At the end of April, conditions were right for putting the seedlings in the ground. I say this as though it was a matter-of-fact kind of thing to do. Actually, I was out of my skin with excitement. Those little seedlings had given me a huge sense of accomplishment. Things had actually grown. The kit contained small packets of soil held together by material that would go in the ground with the seedlings. I had chosen mostly vegetables and a few flowers.

When I first started gardening, I was reluctant to start my plantings from seeds. I think it was a matter of faith—or lack of it. I looked at seeds skeptically. How could such tiny little bits of whatever grow to be something real to look at, like a beautiful flower, much less something to eat? I have a children's book called *A Seed is a Promise*. I thought of the book as I placed the seeds in the soil, covered them gently, and watered hopefully.

On this day, I'm putting morning glory seedlings in the ground. Years ago, our friend Barbara looked at the fence by our garden area and said, "I can see morning glories along this fence." She said it as she says most everything: thoughtfully and with a smile. When it comes to gardening, I try to remember whatever Barbara says. The garden she tends at her Massachusetts home is breathtakingly beautiful with poppies, delphinium, and many other flowering plants that burst with color. Barbara's husband, Dick, goes to church on Sunday. She goes to her garden.

One year, with Barbara's suggestion in mind, I bought young morning glory plants. It took some time to untangle them from one another, but they survived the separation procedure and were treated to their own space in the ground along the fence. Our friend was right. It is a lovely sight.

I want to move these new little plants to the ground before they get too big and begin to entwine. I feel rather protective of them. They have fulfilled their promise so far. All I did was put seeds in the soil, and what I have now looks exactly like a morning glory seedling. Nature impresses and excites me.

Today I'm not alone in the garden. The seeds fulfilled their promise and grew into plants just as new life came into our family. With the birth of our first grandchild, a new generation has begun. She's with me in the garden, asleep in her stroller. Her little six-week-old feet peek out from under a lightweight blanket. A Japanese red maple shades her. The tree was a gift from a friend to our daughter, Kimberly, for her baby blessing. One day, I'll tell baby Madison such things. Kim will be "Ciocie" to Madison, the Polish word for "aunt." (Ciocie rhymes with touchy, as in sensitive, like the Ciocie's in our family.) I wonder if Madison or others will be interested in the family history that is in and around our yard.

When our own kids - Kim, Jeremy and Zac - were young, we had a horse. It happened that the family of Jeremy's friend, Josh, learned about a horse that needed a home. They have a great love for horses, and keep their horse on their property behind the house. The horse they told Jeremy about wasn't for sale. It was up for adoption. Free.

When it came to pets, we didn't say no to our kids often, but we didn't know anything about the care of horses. And while we had the two acres required by the town code, we didn't have a barn. But we said yes to the horse, and Tom built a barn. I loved it. It was small, but big enough for a good-sized stall and tack room.

We purchased a saddle, blanket, and all the rest of the necessities. We bought grain and hay, buckets for food and water, special rakes for picking up manure, and shampoo for his mane. We found a farrier for shoeing him. He even had a dentist.

And then, of course, we needed barn cats, whose job it would be to keep rodents away from the grain. The three cats that lived in the house with us didn't quite qualify for the job.

Tom built a place in the tack room for the barn cats to sleep, hang out, and feel important. It was an impressive cat condo. Murphy, one of the cats, is still with us. His brother, Cosmo, died, but we have some lovely pictures of him taken mostly in the garden. That's where he liked to be, especially when we were there. And somehow, though in a terribly weakened condition, that's where he took himself to die.

Another investment for the horse, and probably the most important one, was the fence. Once that was on the property, we were ready to welcome our "free" horse. His name was Bozley.

After school, Zac, Jeremy, and Kim were responsible for cleaning up the piles of manure. Like good siblings, they were intent on keeping everything fair, so whoever got out to the paddock first would count out the piles of manure, divide by three, and pick up exactly that amount. We learned that one horse can provide plenty of fertilizer. That was one reason why, years later, we chose this particular area for the garden. It's been fertilized rather well.

After Bozley died we boarded a few other horses. They had almost an acre to use, but they spent most of their time close to the barn in this small paddock, the paddock that is now the garden.

On a weekend visit, a college friend of Jeremy's painted a sign on a piece of scrap wood that says: "Paddock Plantings." Here and there, you can find one of Bozley's old horseshoes. Maybe more obvious is the fence gate that he would gnaw. If you didn't know about Bozley, it would just look like any old beat up wooden gate.

I like the different buckets we had for the horse. Two big sturdy ones used for mucking, one blue, one red, have rope handles that made dragging them across the paddock manageable. We had smaller buckets that we used for the grain and water. They're made very practically with one side that's flat. When they hang over the fence post the flat side rests right up against the fence. We had more of those buckets than we needed. So, a lot of times, a bucket was left hanging upside down over a post and went unused for quite awhile. Bees once decided that one of the dark hanging buckets made a perfect place for a hive. The marks on the post make it look like a piece of wood that was abused. But it wasn't. The bees used it as building material.

I'm sure Madison will see pictures of Bozley, and she'll certainly see his gravesite. It just looks like a flowerbed on the front lawn. There's a post in the center of the bed with his name hanging from it. One of the kids made it in shop class. Birds often sat on Bozley's back, apparently looking for insects, so a birdhouse sits on top of the post. It just seemed appropriate.

When we knew that Bozley was going to die, we had two options for his body. For a fee of $50, we could take it to the town dump, or we could hope that no one would notice and we could bury him illegally on our property. Bozley was a pet who we all loved. We would bury him.

The hole required was large, so we had a guy with a backhoe come over to dig it. The vet who had taken care of Bozley said he would arrange to be here at the same time. He would give Bozley the injection that would put him out of his misery.

Another decision had to be made: We could walk him down into the hole for the injection or let him stand at the edge where he would fall down gently into it. Emotionally, we couldn't walk him down there, and he didn't fall gently. Some things just don't go as planned.

We learned a lot about horses. And, of course, we learned there's no such thing as a free horse. But we had a good time with Bozley, and we were glad to give him a home and some comfort as he got old.

In what used to be the tack room with the saddle, blanket, helmets, brushes, and other such things, we now store large and small garden tools and supplies. For a long time, I could still pick up the scent of a horse.

Now, the paddock area has the scent of mint that grows undisciplined there. And there are lilacs.

Madison will call me "Babcia," but she'll hear about other Babcias; Tom's mother and his grandmother. His mother, Louise, was born in May. She called lilacs her flowers. When she passed in early 2006, I bought three lilac bushes. The plan is that each one of our kids will take one to his or her own properties.

My mother, whom our kids called "Nana," died the following fall. A pear tree grows not far from the garden in her memory. It was a gift to me from friends at the Mattituck Florist.

That same year, on Christmas day, my younger sister Liz died. Childhood friends whom I've stayed in touch with over the years, Marilyn and Susan, gave us a small holly bush in Liz's memory that we planted by the house.

It's hard to imagine the evergreen to the left of the barn that now measures about 40 feet tall was one of our Christmas trees. I do wish we had noted somewhere the year that the giant tree stood a mere six feet tall in our small living room. We didn't really have a sense of family history when we put it in the ground. It was a bit of a chore to plant those balled trees. If you didn't plan ahead and dig a hole before the ground froze, you faced a challenging task.

The huge trees at the end of our driveway were only about five feet tall when we planted them. They grew so big that their lower branches were in the way when we parked a car near the house. One spring years ago, we went on a garden tour of local properties. It was a great way to spend a day, and we found the remedy to the problem of obtrusive branches. Tom cut off all the lower branches, and we started a bed of shade plants.

Often we were too reluctant to make financial investments in landscaping. So, for a few years, our shade-plant beds were more mulch than plants. Not so today. Today, they're almost full and are quite lush with large hastas, Solomon's seal, some vinca groundcovering, and delicate, beautifully-scented lilies of the valley.

We found the lilies of the valley in the woods where Zac once rented a house. There's a sweet little song about lilies of the valley that Tom mentioned for some reason on one of our first dates. I asked him to sing it. He did. I liked it and wanted to learn it. So I asked him to sing it again—and again. I loved his voice and his willingness to appease me. I still love his voice.

For a long while, I hadn't heard him sing very much at all. But now, when he holds Madison, I often hear him sing her a made-up little tune. Sometimes I think that if I were ever really, really sick, what I would want most would be for Tom to sing for me. If that happens, I hope he appeases me again.

My family lived in Queens until I was in second grade. I remember walking home from kindergarten, singing as I walked home alone. It was a song about spring: "First, I hear the robin sing. Then, I hear the blue bird's call. But yellow, yellow daffodil, I love you best of all." All these years later, I still think of that song when I see our daffodils make their early spring appearance. Besides being a sign of spring's arrival, I think of them as a symbol of strength. They are, of course, among the first to proclaim that new life awaits us yet again. And they often have to endure the return of harsh weather conditions. But they're strong, so they survive. Their strength alone would not be enough. They survive also because their stalks are flexible. I'm reminded of a card that I once framed for myself that says, "Blessed are the flexible for we shall not be bent out of shape."

The house we live in today in Laurel is the same one we purchased on our second anniversary back in 1977. The people who built the house and lived in it for four years probably wouldn't recognize it.

When Zac, our firstborn, was a baby, we were still picking strawberries from the patches the original owners had cultivated. I have a picture of me and Zac in the strawberries. He was almost a year old, sitting up in the white plastic tub we bathed him in as an infant. I was in my blue jean overalls and a sleeveless shirt. A brimmed hat covered my red hair. We were picking and eating the berries.

I feel a sense of awe today as I watch over Zac and Michelle's daughter, Madison, napping in her carriage in that same spot. I check often to make sure she's shaded from the bright sun. I wonder if her sleep is better in some way because birds are singing nearby.

I'm older now, and I hope to live long enough to be considered old. Maybe I'll bore Madison or other grandchildren, repeating stories they've heard before about the barn, the trees, the plants around the property, and the family connections tied to them. I am keenly aware of my many blessings. One is being healthy enough to spend a morning or any time working in the garden. Another is this grandchild. On this morning, this spring, I know morning glory.

June 2009

"It is more fun to talk with someone who doesn't use long, difficult words but rather short, easy words like 'What about lunch?'"
—*A.A. Milne,* Winnie-the-Pooh

Playgroup

I recently spoke with a mom whose full-time job is to be home with her baby. Although she is terribly sleep deprived, she seemed fine. I thought of myself during the years I had that job. I don't know if it showed when I related to others, but I was seldom fine. Lots of times I felt overwhelmed, and often, I felt isolated and lonely.

My closest women friends and my sisters were either far away in other states or in different stages of their lives. My mother was in Florida. At that time, phone companies made daytime calling for casual conversations difficult. Long-distance telephone calls were expensive. Later in the day, calls were less expensive, but I didn't need someone to talk to later in the day. I wanted to talk during the day.

I had always wanted to be two things: a teacher and a mom. When I had imagined motherhood, I imagined being the one who was with my kids most of the time. I hadn't given any thought to daycare or a full-time babysitter. But this was the late 1970s and early 1980s. So many women I knew went back to work after having babies—not years later, but within a year or two. It seemed the smart thing to do, particularly in the school district where I worked at the time.

The William Floyd School District in Shirley, New York, was a fast-growing district where change was the norm—in administration, teaching staff, and instructional programs. The change was stimulating but exhausting. In the four years that I taught children with learning disabilities there, I made a grade-level change each year. My commute from home took 50 minutes—not a bad drive in decent weather. On my ride home, I'd take Sunrise Highway and exit in Westhampton for Old Riverhead Road to the North Fork of Long Island. A few times, while tired, I missed my exit and had to go as far as Hampton Bays, about another eight miles, before I could turn back toward home.

During my last year teaching at Floyd, I was pregnant with our first child. I remember falling asleep one night at the dining room table on a pile of papers I needed to grade. When I woke up, fear struck. Could I do the two jobs women I worked with were doing: teaching and parenting? Most of them seemed to do it quite well. They'd often take a year off, returning to the same grade level they'd taught in previous years. But one woman returned to her second-grade class just six weeks after having her baby. She asked a lot of her body, and the strain showed.

For every year that I taught in a public school, my federal student loan decreased 10 percent. The William Floyd School District was designated an economically deprived district, and that designation changed the 10 percent decrease to 15 percent.

I'd grown up in that school district. It's where I attended elementary school. I felt connected there, but I couldn't convince myself that returning to teaching full time was best for our family.

Tom and I decided that I'd stay home with our kids. While it was exactly what I wanted to do, I struggled with the decision. Even decades later, I wondered if I'd made the right choice. We supplemented Tom's teaching salary with a small alternative-energy business that we'd started with another couple. Tom climbed rooftops on weekends, installing solar panels. And he cut through ceilings and rooftops for the chimneys of the wood- and coal-burning stoves that our business sold and installed.

He prepared to leave one Saturday morning. We'd had two of our three children by this time, and another long day alone with our two boys lay ahead of me. Loneliness had sapped my energy. I blurted out something that I must have been thinking about for a while: "I'm going to start a playgroup," I said.

Tom looked surprised and wondered aloud, "Who's gonna come?"

I couldn't answer that. I had no idea. I just knew I had to find a remedy for my feelings of isolation.

Tom taught in an all-male science department, and I knew the wives of his co-workers. Some were home with kids. I felt comfortable with two or three of them and invited them over for coffee. Bring your preschoolers, I'd told them. Wednesday morning. Ten 'til noon.

The women came over, I believe, just to be nice. They didn't need the company. They came with their small children, but they had school-aged kids, too. They'd been part of the community for years and knew lots of people. They weren't lonely—and they were busy. They didn't say so, but I could tell that a playgroup would almost get in their way.

But the women each knew someone else who might be interested in a playgroup, and those women knew others, and someone had just met a woman new to the area. Before I knew it, 12 women and their preschoolers came to our house every Wednesday morning, and I loved it.

I had asked that each of the children bring a toy to share so my kids weren't the only ones sharing their toys. I asked the moms to bring a healthy snack to share with all the kids. I'd put on a big pot of coffee, I told them. No one ever mentioned bagels, buttered rolls, or muffins. We seemed to all want the same thing: just coffee and company—and not necessarily in that order.

Today we have a nice backyard with a tennis court, a garden, and a grassy area. Back when the kids were little, the yard was almost bare. I don't even remember if we had a swing set. I do remember a sandbox. The kids were always involved in play. The littlest ones stayed close to the moms. When hungry, they nursed. When the weather wasn't good for outside play, we gathered in the basement. One of the stoves that we sold warmed the basement, which was finished enough so it was adequate play space.

During those years, many of us used playpens. One Wednesday morning, one of the babies played happily in the playpen. I thought she might enjoy another toy, so I checked with her mom, Jan, whose Southern accent complimented her easygoing manner. Jan, upbeat and fun, had moved to eastern Long Island from Florida. I knew her husband, Artie, from our high school days together at Mercy High School in Riverhead. I never did find out exactly how and when they'd met.

When I'd asked Jan if her daughter would like another toy, Jan looked at her little girl and then at me and said, "My daddy always told me, 'If it ain't broke, don't fix it.'"

It was the first time I'd heard the expression. I've heard it often since then, although not quite the way Jan would say it.

The group changed when a family moved away, when one of the women brought someone new, and when more babies were born, including our daughter. Sometimes playgroup time became a baby shower.

One mom, Barbara, and her husband, Tim, had adopted their first child. A couple of years later, she became pregnant, and her birth experience inspired me to write her a poem. Part of it went like this:

We playgroup moms were happy and excited,
Barbara was pregnant, nothing less than delighted.
She once asked the doctor, "About what size will it be?"
"Oh, an average-sized baby," he said, assuredly.
"That's nice," she thought and did what she could
to prepare for the new one, like any wise mother would.
They went to the classes, had the layette all aired.
Not wanting, of course, to be caught unprepared.
But Barbara, oh, Barbara, what a surprise for you!
You gave birth to little Steven—then discovered there were two!
"Yipes," said Tim, "If only we knew."
"He's kidding," thought Barbara. "There aren't two."
But then there was Lauren, precious and small.
Twins! Three kids! Our very best to you all.

The Wednesday morning playgroup gatherings lasted for about four years. Kids turned school-aged. Some moms returned to work. Some families moved. Some returned to their home states, like Sharon's family, which returned to Illinois.

Tom and I did further renovations to the basement, including upgrading the heating system and painting the barn-board walls white with a red accent. I hired two early-childhood teachers, Jane and Debbie, and, for 10 years, I used the basement space for The Cat and the Fiddle Nursery School three mornings a week. Our youngest, Kimberly, was in my first class. I loved it. I was still running The Cat and the Fiddle when we hosted a high-school exchange student from Paraguay. He called it "The Little School."

Sharon and I have kept in touch over the decades. She's more than 10 years younger than I am, and we're different in many ways, but we bonded back in those early parenting years. I have great respect and love for her.

A few years ago, Sharon celebrated her 50th birthday with a trip back to New York. She and her husband, John, stopped by our house. More so than usual, I wanted everything to be impossibly perfect when

Sharon and John visited. Their youngest son had died less than a year earlier, and I wanted to come together and be comfortable with a good home-cooked meal.

The day became complicated when our daughter, Kim, had an ulcerative colitis flare-up. It was worrisome, but she was OK. I let go of the "perfect visit" idea, and we enjoyed Sharon and John's company over good takeout. We updated each other on what we knew of the old playgroup families and how we had all been saddened by two early deaths: Barbara had been strong through a long struggle with cancer. Jan's death was sudden. Both women left behind three kids before they'd all reached adulthood.

The visit with Sharon and John was the first time I'd ever seen Sharon wear makeup. It might have been the first time she saw me in makeup, too. When I was younger and busy with my kids, I was just glad to have showered, dressed, and brushed my teeth. Maybe in another decade or so I'll put aside the makeup. Maybe I'll go back to being comfortable and content with having showered, dressed, and brushed my teeth.

I remembered Sharon as such a refreshing personality with her Midwestern accent, flawless fair skin, pretty blond hair, and her easy laugh and relaxed manner. That was all apparent still, but so were life experiences that had changed us.

In some ways, I suppose, "playgroup" was another name for "support group." We were a group of average moms, but we were smart, too. I say "smart" because when we met each Wednesday morning, we stayed away from controversial subjects. We gave ourselves, and each other, what we needed at the time. No heated discussions. No gooey coffee cake or donuts. We gave each other our company, a little time, and some laughs.

"Bring something for the snack table and a toy to share. I'll put on coffee." It was simple. And it served us well.

November 2013

"... The flowering tree was the living center of the hoop, and the circle of the four quarters nourished it. The east gave peace and light, the south gave warmth, the west gave rain, and the north with its cold and mighty wind gave strength and endurance."

Black Elk - Oglala Sioux

Mandalas

Sue and I once took for granted our time together. That was almost 50 years ago, when we were college roommates at Long Island University, now Stony Brook University at Southampton. Now, it's a treat if we see each other, in person, once a year. I'm still on the east coast, but Sue is on the other side of the country, near Portland, Oregon. She's an unconventional thinker, wise, spiritual, and one of the funniest people I know.

Typical of close friendships, nothing's ever too mundane or too bizarre for us to talk about. We stay in touch with e-mails and occasional phone calls. We also like to Skype, that is, use computer software to make video calls. Tom and I use it to see our baby granddaughter, Leah, in Delaware. That's something grandparents typically do with video calls.

Sue and I use it for lengthy face-to-face conversations, usually over her breakfast and my lunch. Every now and then, we include what's not so typical: a few minutes of meditation time. We fix ourselves some tea, each light a candle, and one, or both of us, say some words to set our intentions.

The practice of meditation used to be thought of as unconventional, but its benefits have become widely known and accepted and its practice, more mainstream. At one time, I might have timidly asked my gastroenterologist, "Do you think meditation would help?" Today, I know it's a suggestion he might bring up first.

Dusting off my bookshelves recently, I came across a book called *Mandala: Journey to the Center* by Bailey Cunningham. The inside inscription reads: "To my friend Mary Ellen, who is a living mandala.

Happy 60th birthday. Love, Sue." It was only a short time before receiving that book that I'd become familiar with mandalas. Otherwise, I would have questioned, "I'm a living *what*?"

Sue has some health issues that challenge her, so when we see each other, I make the flight out to Oregon. She's still the college roommate who nudges me gently into new territory of thinking, to wonder with her about things out of the ordinary.

During one week-long visit to her home, we started each day by creating mandalas. After our breakfast—her tea, and my coffee—we cleared the kitchen table and spread out some basic art supplies: paper, colored pencils, and a compass. Since Sue is a confident artist and I'm good at stick figures, I had some head work to do before I could sit at the same table and do artwork with her. My trust in her and her experience working with other non-artists helped.

I knew what mandalas, generally, looked like, but I had no idea how much I'd enjoy our daily morning practice of drawing a circle and filling in the space with designs and colors. I came to learn the truth of what Sue said our first morning of mandala–making: "Mandalas are everywhere." And I learned that what we played around with at her kitchen table was an art form that's been around for millennia.

Mandalas have been found in all cultures, as well as all religions, throughout history. Christians used them to express visions and religious beliefs. The Aztec people used them both as timekeepers and for religious expression. Native Americans created medicine wheels and sand mandalas. In the Jewish tradition, when a couple marries, they sign a contract called a "ketubah." Since about the 14th century, the mandala design has been used to decorate ketubahs. Our son Jeremy and his wife, Jess, have their ketubah—a treasured and meaningful work of art—hanging on their dining room wall.

Some mandalas were made of giant stone and have survived for centuries. Others are made to deliberately lack permanence. In some parts of India, women use mandalas as part of a daily ritual. They make them on the ground with chalk powder, grain, or flower petals. The hope is that the mandalas will bring good fortune and protection to their home, family, and harvest.

"Mandala" is a Sanskrit word, the ancient language of India. Generally, it means "circle." The round shape represents wholeness. The designs and the colors that we put in and around our circle can reflect how we're feeling at a given time. I love the mandalas I've drawn, but I would bet most anything that I'm the only person who would feel that way about them. Sue made an exquisite mandala that I was glad to see she framed and put on her wall. My mandalas are in a 5-inch by 7-inch notebook of unlined pages. They speak to me. They have calmed me and even inspired me.

Not all mandalas are circular. After the United States was attacked in September 2001, the Dalai Lama requested that Tibetan Buddhists from around the world take part in healing our country through meditation, prayer ceremonies, and the sacred healing arts. At the Smithsonian's Sackler Gallery in Washington, D.C., monks created a seven-foot-square mandala. For two weeks, 20 monks worked in shifts to complete the mandala made from millions of grains of powdered, colored marble. And then, to symbolize the impermanence of existence, the monks destroyed it. They dispersed the sand in the Potomac River with the belief that the water carried the sand's healing energy throughout the world.

In the early 1900s, Carl Jung, the noted psychoanalyst, wrote about mandalas in his book *Mandala Symbolism*. Between 1918 and 1919, Jung had been a senior commanding officer of a prisoner-of-war camp. He wrote:

> *I sketched every morning in a notebook a small circular drawing, a mandala, which seemed to correspond to my inner situation at the time. . . . To be sure, at first I could only dimly understand them; but they seemed to me highly significant, and I guarded them like precious pearls.*

I understand that guarded feeling Jung had about his mandalas. I feel that way about some of mine.

At Sue's suggestion, I've titled the mandalas I've done. The titles that come to mind often surprise me and tend to be revealing. I have one called "Staying Open." I don't remember what was going on at the time, but it's likely I was in need of some prodding to keep an open mind, an open heart, or both.

Later, in his professional work, Jung often used mandalas with his patients. He said creating mandalas gives people a sense of calmness. Before my younger sister Liz died of cancer, she lived with schizophrenia.

She was a gentle, loving person, but there were times when she could be combative, making conversations challenging. One day while we talked on the phone long distance, I decided I would work on a mandala. I knew, at best, I could only control my part of the conversation. If the conversation turned negative, I wanted to stay centered and keep some emotional distance. Instead of getting irritated, I was able to be a calm listener.

I took my mandala pad and colored pencils out on an airplane flight once. I was traveling to visit a friend who was dealing with a serious illness. She was on strong medication that caused her to be high strung and more intense than usual, so I felt some anxiety about the visit. I had a window seat, which allowed me a bit of privacy. I took out my mandala pad and colored pencils, and made a calming, soft-colored mandala. The title of that one, "The Calm Before the Storm," proved to be prophetic. At the end of each frenzied day, I was glad to have my pad and pencils and a relaxing activity.

My husband Tom teaches physics. He loves the subject, reads about it for pleasure, and, occasionally, engages me in some physics talk. I can chuckle at a joke like, "You know why you can't trust an atom? Because they make up everything." My mandala book from Sue has a section called "Science and Nature." I was particularly glad to share with Tom the references to physics. The mandala pattern is everywhere in the natural world. Some suggest that's why we're drawn to it. The blossoms of flowers, spider webs, the ripple made when a drop of water lands on still water, the atom: They're all mandala patterns.

When the week Sue had introduced me to creating mandalas had come to an end, we'd said our emotional goodbyes at the Portland International Airport. It was time for me to head home to Long Island. My long day of travel had begun. I don't mind traveling alone, but it does take a little more energy. At the airport, I focused on my travel details. I checked my luggage, put my pocketbook over one shoulder and my carry-on bag over the other. I looked at the latest information about my flight and connecting flights, put my boarding pass where I'd find it again, and located a coffee shop, a restroom, and the direction to my departing gate.

It wasn't long before I felt weary and somewhat gloomy that another visit with Sue was a whole year away, and then I saw and heard something that caused me to stop moving and quiet my thoughts. My mother had a saying she would use to express someone's joy: "She thought she died and went to heaven." For a split second, I wondered if I had died, gone to heaven, and missed the drama of it all.

There, in the center of the vast airport corridor, sat a woman wearing a long, softly flowing dress, playing a harp. I moved closer. As I listened, I felt the muscles on my face and in my stomach relax and my shoulders drop. I wanted to stay and listen for awhile, but I had to pay attention to time. Nearby, there was a small table with some CDs on it. It was the music of this harpist, Shawndeya. I purchased one. It would remind me of the early morning activities I had shared with Sue during the week. I didn't know it then, but the CD would also become perfect naptime music for grandchildren. The CD is simply called *Mandala*. Sometimes I love the way the universe times things.

Occasionally, I think about something Sue posted on Facebook one New Year's Day: "Buckle your seat belts, fellow humans. We're in for another ride around the sun." For the most part, I'm happy to be taking the ride. But, whether I'm on the back of Tom's and my tandem, riding a bus in bad weather, or one of more than seven billion earth-travelers, I have to fight the impulse to be a nervous passenger.

I tend to want to talk to some almighty being and say, "Hey, God, Goddess. You know me, and you know I don't like scary rides. The ones I've been on already haven't been as bad as some I've heard about. By comparison, mine are like being on a glider swing, so I'm not complaining. It's not that I thought I'd influence some plan. I just like staying in touch."

I think about us buckling up for the ride, cushioning ourselves for the bumps, protecting ourselves from the jolts. I guess, to some extent, we all strive to do that. The woman half a world away from me creates a mandala on the ground from flower petals with hopes of protecting her family, home, and harvest.

The sand mandalas and others that illustrate impermanence both intrigue me and haunt me. I like things as they are. Loved ones, safe. A home, pretty. A garden. Music. Laughter. Books. Grandchildren. Pets. Food. Wine. Friends. Sunsets. The beach. Family. Body parts, working.

Such great care goes into creating a sand mandala, much like life itself. It's hard for me to fathom planning so precisely and laboring so meticulously over something that's intended not to last. I think of some things I've created—a quilted Christmas tree skirt, a knitted scarf, the design of pictures hanging on a wall. Part of their pleasure is that I get to enjoy them repeatedly. I can accept laboring for hours over a big meal and seeing that come to an end. But the impermanence of life, that's a raw truth that's hard to live with.

So, I go to my garden. I see there's fall work to do. But I can ignore that, as I enjoy the lovely late bloomers. I decide to choose one that reflects the most perfect mandala I can find and bring it in the house.

I love this time of year. And I love the look of a perfect daisy in full bloom.

October 2013

With Sue in Oregon, at the Portland Arboretum, I
photographed this spider web, a natural mandala.

September

September is a beautiful month, but over the years, I've experienced it with mixed feelings.

Growing up in New York, September meant the start of the school year. All of the fuss and worry about who has which teacher, the courses, the book bags, the clothes, the friends, the ones who used to be friends, the bus schedule, the planning, wanting to start out on the right foot, wanting to not start at all. Ah, yes, September.

There's an old song, "September Song," from the 1938 musical *Knickerbocker Holiday*. A variety of artists, including Jimmy Durante, Sarah Vaughan and Willie Nelson have sung the words of this wistful pop standard:

> *Oh, it's a long, long while, from May to December.*
> *But the days grow short when you reach September.*

Of all the many renditions, it was probably Jimmy Durante's that I grew up hearing. The song goes on to say,

> *When the autumn weather turns the leaves to flame,*
> *One hasn't got time for the waiting game.*

Lyricist, Maxwell Anderson, used a year of a life as a metaphor for the span of a lifetime. He writes of days that "dwindle down to a precious few."

I think of my brother Al. He was married only a couple of years with a six-month-old daughter. He died in the month of January. I think of him because his time, his days, dwindled down way too soon — and because "September Song" was his favorite. I wouldn't have known that, but my brother John told me. He and Al were close in age and good buddies.

September anxiety this year is different than in any of my earlier years. I'm not enrolled as a student anywhere. My job doesn't start until October. My three kids are all adults. But it's 2008—a presidential election year in the United States.

I enjoy history, and I took a couple of political science courses in college. The little that I know about the lives of our past presidents I find fascinating. I love the insight presidential historians give us into the lives of the people who have led this country. It's not always flattering stuff, but it's always interesting.

My father also died the January that my brother Al died. They worked together on a tugboat that went down in the Long Island Sound during a storm. I was 10. My mother, who was pregnant with her ninth child, was left alone with eight kids. After three years, she bravely entered the workforce, managing to get a job about 15 miles from home in Patchogue Town Hall.

For almost 20 years, she worked in the town clerk's office with the same group of women. While the staff of women in the office basically remained the same, the person in the town clerk's position often changed. Each election time, the women either hoped voters would throw the bum out or hoped the best man for the job would stay on the job. Sometimes things didn't work out the way my mother and her co-workers thought it ought to, and they mourned the loss of a good public servant and a good boss. For better or worse, the name on the pencils, the letterhead, and the door changed.

The women in the office did their same jobs year after year. But after an election year, if they had a newly-elected boss, they had to teach him his job. Depending on his personality, it was either a dreaded time or a time filled with hope. It's what we kids heard about over the dinner table, and it's what I remember about politics growing up.

The first president I remember is Dwight D. Eisenhower. He was a popular Republican president. At least, I think he was popular. I never heard anyone in our house say anything bad about him. He looked like a nice guy and, as a kid, I could read the signs that said "I like Ike." Ike's wife, Mamie, looked like she'd be a sweet aunt.

What we felt for Eisenhower was nothing compared to the feelings that we had for John F. Kennedy. We didn't just like him, we loved him. And we loved his beautiful wife and their adorable kids. I wanted to exercise because he wanted us to be fit. I wanted to hear him speak to the press because I liked to hear him talk. People were joining the Peace Corp. We didn't know it at the time, but Kennedy's days were growing short in September. There were precious few.

I'm doing what I can this September to stave off anxiety about the presidential election. I refuse to preach to the choir this time like a lot of us did four years ago, sharing e-mail messages with like-minded voters. I want to reach people who think that their vote doesn't matter, who have no interest in politics, who feel totally disconnected from the whole process. I want to encourage them and talk to them about those who suffered just to get the right to vote.

I've never been very good at what I'm trying to do this fall. I've been passionate about elections before, but when I tried to speak to someone about why, I got all tight, tense, and shrill.

I want to believe that we'll be OK, no matter how it turns out, but I don't. I need a person to lead with a new vision. That September anxiety is at its peak, and it's worse than the school year when I wore all of my new clothes the first week of school, even though they were wool and we were having Indian Summer. And it's worse than the grade school years when we had split sessions, being assigned to either a morning or afternoon school day, and austerity budgets that didn't provide bussing. We didn't like those times, but we got through them.

I haven't liked the last eight years at all. Politically speaking, that is. In my personal life, on the other hand, I've been blessed. Not free of challenges, but not wrought with devastation either. Oftentimes, when I look at my beautiful yard, I imagine a woman in Iraq who may have once enjoyed a garden, too. I know it's true that, even before we invaded her country, fear—and even horror—at times filled her life and the lives of her fellow Iraqis. The Iraqis needed help, but they didn't need what they got, and neither did we.

"Oh, the days dwindle down to a precious few." In a couple of weeks, I'll be part of a group of volunteers who help with the voting process. We'll walk through neighborhoods, knocking on doors, talking to residents about voter registration. I can't imagine anything more satisfying as a citizen than to help others participate in democracy by voting. This isn't something that I've ever done before. But, as the song says, "one hasn't got time for the waiting game."

2008

Albie and me, in 1947, in front of my grandfather's house, our home, on 53rd Avenue in Elmhurst. Albie was 11 years old. He had 11 more years left.

"What bound people together was so fragile."
—*Paul Russell,* The Coming Storm

Close Enough

Ah, it's spring 2010. Here in the northeast, it was a cold, snowy winter. But through the storms and blizzards, our neighbors were there for us, enabling us to get in and out of our driveway as needed. I guess for some people, those biblical words, "Love thy neighbor as thyself," can be challenging. And while I'm not sure I understand precisely their full meaning, I do know that my husband, Tom, and I appreciate our really good neighbors.

On one side of us is a young single guy who lives in a spacious house. He's past his 20s and even his 30s, but we still think of him as The Young Guy Next Door. A student from Tom's early teaching days, he is generous with the use of his tractor, other large equipment, and even a roadway that's on his property.

The first year that he moved next door, he invited us to his Super Bowl party. "Stop in for a beer," he had suggested. "Anytime from 11, on."

I thought we must have heard wrong. But by 11 a.m., more than 50 pickup trucks lined the street. We appreciated his friendly gesture, but we skipped the party. Instead, we stayed in our flannels and poured ourselves second cups of coffee.

On the other side of us is a couple our age. Although we have been neighbors for more than 30 years, we're not what you would call "close" but "close enough." We don't really get together socially, except for special occasions, like our children's weddings. We do often enjoy lengthy conversations on our shared driveway. And although we never talk politics, I think it is safe to say that we've probably never voted for the same people.

When our kids—Kimberly, Jeremy, and Zachary—were ages 4, 7, and 9, Tom left his teaching career for about a decade or so, becoming a partner in a computer software company. His work required long hours six days a week. Sometimes he had to be away from home for an overnight trip or for several days. I was busy with all that was involved in family life, as well as my part-time work running a pre-school in our renovated basement. I don't remember feeling fearful when he was away, but, once, I did call our good neighbor, Ken, for help.

Early one evening, the kids and I were relaxed, watching TV together. When a field mouse raced across the room from one end to the other, I let out a scream as I pulled my feet up and huddled on the couch. I think my reaction alarmed the kids more than the mouse did, maybe because upstairs in their bedrooms they had caged pets that resembled this critter. We had always shared our home with at least two cats, but, apparently, they were too comfortable to be interested in some brazen rodent.

I was the adult in the room. I had to be brave—at least brave enough to get off the couch and do something. I called Ken.

Within minutes, he arrived with a mousetrap. And then, he took his kindness a step further, saying, "If you hear it go off, call me. I'll come over and take care of it." And he did. I thought it was important for our kids to feel a sense of security with their mom or dad. My exception: dealing with mice.

When our kids were little, they would watch the same movies over and over again. I watch a movie I've already seen only if I've forgotten that I already saw it. But recently, I have intentionally watched a movie a second, and even, a third time: *Mamma Mia*. There's no violence or heavy suspense, just fun and good music. I've watched it repeatedly and dance to its soundtrack often. My one-year-old granddaughter delights in my routine, and I delight in hamming it up for her.

But there's a scene toward the end of the movie when I sit down, soak it up, and get teary-eyed each time. Meryl Streep's character, Donna, laments her relationship with her daughter in a song called "Slipping Through my Fingers." I think of my own daughter—and the daughter I was—when I hear her sing, "Do I really see what's in her mind? Each time I think I'm close to knowing, she keeps on growing."

I struggled through some difficult conversations with my mother. We had deep love for each other, but I can't say we were close. It's not that I feel we needed to be. But we needed more than we had. We needed to be close enough so that when we needed to have tough conversations, we had the words, some history, and a smidgeon of comfort.

I was out of high school for a year and working as a secretary to a school principal when I realized I wanted to be a teacher. The thought of telling my mother that I wanted to go to college unnerved me. We'd never talked about it, and none of my five older siblings had gone. The tension I felt around the thought of having that conversation at 18 years old was probably equal to what some girls my age felt when they had to tell their mothers they were pregnant. My news should not have been so difficult.

My mother's reaction—considering the stresses of widowhood and financial struggles—I suppose, was reasonable. She expressed concern about where the money would come from. Timidly, I told her that I'd heard about loans I could get and pay back once I had a job. Some of our struggle was about saying words for the first time that hadn't ever been spoken before between us.

In June 2008, our local paper published a series called *Gay on the North Fork*. The writer's 14-year-old daughter had asked her, "Would you hate me if I were gay?" The writer, Denise Civiletti, assured her daughter that she would not. Mother and daughter may never need to revisit that issue, but if they do, they've had the advantage of a close enough relationship for the words to have been spoken aloud already between them.

For 10 years, I ran my pre-school with two other teachers, Jane and Debbie, assisting me. We had lots of fun with three- and four-year-olds, but I wondered whether the children all had close-enough people in their lives. Each year I invited a police officer to talk to the children about good and bad touches—and what to do about bad touches. Of course, parents signed permission forms and I also invited them to attend. Of all the experiences that we offered preschoolers at The Cat & The Fiddle Nursery School, I still feel this was one of the most important.

I remember a little guy named Rodney. Separating from his mom on schooldays was difficult for him. He did OK for a while, but then he would have an outburst when least expected. I sat in a preschooler-sized chair, which put my ear and Rodney's mouth at the same height. He used to come up next to me and let out a blood-curdling scream that would truly make my eardrum quiver. When I often need the TV louder than others watching with me, I think of little Rodney.

I didn't worry about him the way, that I worried about a few others over the years, such as Sandra. She appeared terribly passive and vulnerable. I wanted her to learn to say no and to sound like she meant it. I wanted to equip her in every way possible. My influence was limited, but my hope was that the children's relationships with their parents were close enough for talks that just might be needed some day.

It has been four years since my mother-in-law passed on. My father-in-law, Ed—her husband of more than 60 years—has been to her gravesite innumerable times, sometimes every day. He spends a lot of time with immediate family members, but at 85, he has never talked about his end-of-life wishes. We've had no reason to think that he would ever consider anything other than what's been familiar and traditional in his family. When our daughter, Kim, came home for Thanksgiving last fall, she visited him at his home in Riverhead, just the two of them. Ed hadn't seen Kim in three months, and he had her full attention, talking about topics he hadn't discussed before with anyone else in the family. To the surprise of the rest of us, that included his wish to be cremated. I'm not sure Kim considers herself close with her grandfather, but, apparently, they both feel close enough.

Relationships that fill a need for closeness can even go beyond this life. I've been reading about Rumi, a prophet from the 1200s who was born in what is now Afghanistan. He is considered the greatest mystic of Islam—a tender, tolerant worker of miracles, a healer of body and soul. His goal was to teach people how to live happy lives and to be at peace with God. In Rumi's biography, his son is quoted as saying:

> One day I said to my father, "[F]riends claim that when they do not see you, it causes them pain and their inner joy disappears." My father replied, "Whoever does not feel joyful in my absence does not really know me; the one who really knows me feels happy even without me; he will be suffused with me, with the thought of me, with my thought. . . . Every time, my son, that you find yourself in a state of mystic sweetness, know that this state is me in you. . . . When you look for me, look in the district of joy. . . ."

I believe that would be at least a notch or two up from a close-enough relationship.

The winter storms are over. It's spring now. Of course, there will be other storms, some that neighbors can help with, but not all. There will be more awkward conversations with loved ones. They will express new ideas and share dreams. They will speak words that are hard to say, some that may even hurt my ears.

When things really get to me, I know how to sit with my tears or my prayers or both. I treasure my close relationships where words, emotions, conversations flow easily. But I have also learned to value the relationships that are just close enough.

2010

My husband, Tom, and our neighbor, Ken, clearing our driveway. For better traction, Tom adds his weight to Ken's snow blower. We loved Ken. He was a wonderful neighbor. His death in February 2011 saddened all of us.

"Where there is love, there is life."
—Mahatma Gandhi

Valentine's Day Times 12

I don't know about you, but, over the years, I've experienced the arrival of Valentine's Day with ambivalent feelings. Early on, my husband, Tom, and I had similar feelings about Valentine's Day. We agree with Jon Stewart, host of *The Daily Show*, who once said, "Valentine's Day is oftentimes a, well, it's a manufactured day that really doesn't mean anything."

But, at times, I admit, I felt I was missing out on something. When my kids were little, I loved receiving their handmade valentines. Now, the holiday is stretching in its scope. Some of that is due to a cultural shift. For example, the American Heart Association (AHA) encourages us to think about our real hearts. In February, the AHA takes advantage of all the valentine hearts on display and promotes medical check-ups.

So, I've lightened up my feelings about this made-for-Hallmark day. And although I still agree with Jon Stewart, I don't really mind observing the day, especially now that it's more layered in meaning.

A woman I knew from church years ago surprised me one February. She was single, in her early 40s, and seemed to be extremely independent. I thought of her as a free spirit who would easily resist the superficial. I was rather astonished when she told me about a call she made to an old boyfriend. She didn't have romantic feelings for him, but she invited him to spend the night on February 14. She told me, rather sadly, "I didn't want to be alone that night."

I saw her as eccentric and out of the mainstream—so much so that I would have guessed Valentine's Day would come and go without her ever noticing—but not so. She bought into all the commercial, romantic hype about that one day. And maybe she couldn't help hear the words of comedian, Lewis Black, who shouts almost everything he says: "Valentine's Day: The holiday that reminds you that if you don't have a special someone, you're alone." And maybe that would disturb her enough to take to heart a wisecrack attributed to the actor, Dudley Moore: "I'm always looking for meaningful one-night stands."

After more than 60 years living in this culture, I still can't tell you much at all about the person Saint Valentine. One Internet source claims that 14 martyred saints of ancient Rome were all named Valentine. There's a book, the *Roman Martyrology*, that for February 14, mentions only one Saint Valentine. So, while there were apparently other Valentines who attained sainthood, there is only one who we celebrate in February.

Made up or not, perhaps this holiday serves a good purpose. A friend owns a flower shop, and I'm happy for her when I see her have a successful business day. In our family, February 14 is a special day because it's the day our son Zac and his wife, Michelle, were married.

Quite honestly, I think that if there is a problem with Valentine's Day, it's that it isn't enough. I believe in love. I want to believe it has more energy, more power, and makes more of an impact than hate.

When it comes to people I disdain, sometimes the best I can do is to commit to not hating them or wishing ill on them. It's not a feeling I have toward many people—maybe two. One is a big, loud man who hosts a radio talk show, and one is a man who likes writing on a chalkboard for his TV viewers. They demonize people who don't share their political views with abrasive and outrageous comments.

I could tend toward having an angry knee-jerk reaction to the men, but I try not to. I'd rather consider the Buddhist approach to remain detached and to simply observe.

When my kids were little and used the word "hate"—"I hate lima beans!" "I hate that jerk!"—my rote response was "Save hate for Hitler." I've always felt the word "hate" is a strong word and, like "love," should be used carefully. These men challenge me.

My elderly aunt, a woman of faith, listens to one of them as though he's a man of great wisdom. She likes to keep me up on his latest teachings and warnings. I listen to her soft old voice coming through the phone, and, as gently as I can, I tell her, "Stop. You're almost 95 years old. Why are you putting negative rants in that good head of yours? Change the channel. Say another rosary. Do anything else."

In our church hymnal, there's a section in the back of the book devoted to readings that cover many categories from a variety of authors and world religions. We use the readings commonly in our services for inspiration and comfort. One day, I was feeling particularly troubled by the two men that I mentioned. I checked the hymnal for a relevant reading but couldn't find a category for them. I looked under "outrageous" and "appalling."

The popularity of these two men baffles and saddens me. Their talk all seems to be rooted in anger, hate, and fear. What I know—although I've forgotten it at times—is that I can't respond to them with my own hateful words or even clog my mind with hateful thoughts, for that matter. Prophets throughout the ages have warned us about that and have taught us to do differently.

I remember the late Dr. Leo Buscaglia, a professor, author, and motivational speaker who wrote and spoke extensively about love. He said, "Love is life. And if you miss love, you miss life." If I believe that, then I don't have to disdain people I consider to be wretched characters. I ought to feel sorry for them. I ought to hope and pray, I guess, that they figure out how to stop missing life.

Here's what I'd like to see happen with Valentine's Day, the day we celebrate love. If our culture insists on selling it to us, let's not have just one Valentine's Day. Let's have 12, one every month on the 14th of each month. If we truly believe in love, let's really do it right. Let's celebrate with cards, candy, flowers, and gifts of beautiful jewelry every month. Let's have a different theme each month. We'll keep the traditional theme of romantic love for one of the months, probably February, as it is now. But on the 14th day of the other 11 months, we'll do a Valentine's Day with others in mind.

One month, we'll recognize the people who keep our cities and towns running, along with service people in our lives: mail carriers, valued hairdressers, and so forth. Another month, our cards and gifts will go out to our co-workers, no matter how we feel about them. (Hey, it's the 14th. It's Valentine's Day.) And so, on that day, we'll honor them with our attention, a heart-shaped greeting card, a box of chocolate. Another month, teachers, professors, ministers, and all who instruct us in some way will receive our overt messages of love.

Then, there'll be Happy Immigrant Valentine's Day. Find an immigrant, say, "Happy Valentine's Day," in your language or theirs. The next month, we'll devote the 14th to telling our gay friends and relatives all over the country and the world, "We love and appreciate you. Happy Valentine's Day."

We'll devote the 14th of another month to those who work in the health profession. We could even have a Valentine's Day devoted only to animals, domestic and wild. We would let them know we appreciate the joy, comfort, and companionship they bring us. That would be the month we would hope to see a rise in pet adoptions and neutering.

We'll set aside still another 14th for our human friends, the friends we've had for a lifetime, newer friends, and those whom we'd like to have as friends. We would honor people who serve our country in the political arena—in both parties or no party—on another 14th. And we'll set aside a very special 14th of another month for the men and women who serve our country in the military and their families.

I don't have many poetry books, but what I have, I enjoy. One of my favorites is *The Best-Loved Poems of Jacqueline Kennedy Onassis*, selected and introduced by Caroline Kennedy. Included in the collection is the reading from Corinthians 13: 1-13. It speaks about faith, hope, and love or—depending on the version—faith, hope, and charity. In this version, charity is used, something good to emphasize for one of our 12 Valentine Days.

Combining our modern-day use of the word "charity" with the holiday hype could prove beneficial. Maybe we would fill all the food pantries across the country to the brim, with enough food to last a whole year until Happy Charity Valentine's Day comes around again.

And that makes 12 Valentine Days.

Thus, we fill our entire calendar celebrating love. You can see that I believe we've really been challenged all these years. Celebrating Valentine's Day once a year, only on February 14, has been woefully inadequate. In this life, there is so much love to be expressed, so much love to be recognized, so many who wait to hear from us. There's clearly far too much love for just a one-day celebration.

February 2011

"Cry. Forgive. Learn. Move on.
Let your tears water the seeds of your future happiness."
—Steve Maraboli

The Way They Were

It's May 14, 2010. Nine of us are at a restaurant in Jamesport, Long Island, called the Bayview Inn. If you miss the turn for the restaurant, you meet the beautiful Peconic Bay, head on. We're celebrating my sister and her husband's wedding anniversary. Anne, who was named for my mother, married Mike 50 years ago on this day. We're looking through their wedding album of black-and-white photos. We're laughing, commenting, questioning.

"Look at our hats. They look like Frisbees with bows stuck on them."

"How young Mom looks."

"Where's Billy?"

I'm not sure why—maybe it's the way we're positioned—but our family photo looks sparse to me, although there are eight of us in it. Besides my sister Anne—the bride—there's my mother, Anne, a pretty brunette, who's 42. My brother, John, 21, has been married for a year and half now. Bob is 17. I'm 12 and feeling more awkward than my usual, everyday awkwardness: I'm wearing a bra for the first time. I don't need it, but my undershirt wouldn't have worked with my pretty bridesmaid dress. Liz is 10. It's Patty's birthday. She's 8. Michael is 2½. Billy, 16, ate or drank something that didn't agree with him and missed the family picture.

It's also two-and-a-half years since the tugboat accident that took the lives of my father, Al, and my oldest brother, Albie. My brother John had the honor of walking Anne down the aisle. A couple of years before he died, Albie had gotten married. He and his wife, Eileen, were an attractive couple. Albie was six feet tall and had dark wavy hair, brown eyes, and a slender build. Eileen, an Irish beauty, was much shorter than Albie. She had black wavy hair and green eyes. I don't remember my brother's voice, but I always liked Eileen's. There was, and mostly still is, an appealing lightness to her voice.

Even before they were married, Albie and Eileen showed those of us who were "the little kids" in the family special attention. A Christmas morning photo from 1953 shows me with my younger sisters, Lizzy and Patty, all holding the only dolls I remember us having—gifts from Albie and Eileen.

Albie and Eileen's daughter, Mary Anne, is almost three at the time of my sister's wedding. Neither Eileen nor Mary Anne is in the picture, and they weren't at the wedding.

My mother and Eileen were fond of each other and had a good relationship. It was a relationship that grew stronger after the accident, when Eileen and Mary Anne moved in with us. It was a devastatingly sad time. But having two babies in the house—my brother Michael and niece Mary Anne—distracted us and helped to lift our spirits.

And I loved Eileen like a second mom.

Occasionally, her parents stopped by for coffee and cake. Eileen's parents—John and Bridgette—were Irish immigrants. Everyone called Bridgette by her nickname, "Bridey." John always referred to her as "The Mrs." It didn't matter to me what conversation the adults were having in the kitchen, I always stayed and enjoyed listening to them talk with their thick Irish brogues.

Several months before Anne's wedding, Eileen and Mary Anne moved out of our home. I was getting ready to begin seventh grade. I remember the weekend when Eileen was packing. My sister Liz and I walked behind her, crying as she moved from room to room picking up things to take or just putting things in order. Eileen kept saying, "I'll be back to see you. I'll come next weekend."

My mother tried to explain: "Eileen's young. She needs to make a life of her own now. She can't live with us forever."

It turned out that we didn't see her that following weekend or any other time.

One night, Eileen's brother and sister-in-law came to visit my mother. They talked in whispers in the kitchen. I hid down the hall, trying to hear what they were saying. It was all so confusing.

At Christmastime, Liz and I sat in the living room, writing out cards. We were having a nice time. My mother was nearby, straightening bookshelves. We asked her, "What's Eileen's address?" I'm not sure if she gave us an address. I don't remember hearing anything past Eileen's new last name. That's how we learned she was remarried.

Eileen was 24. Her new husband was divorced with grown kids. I knew who he was. He had been to our house—to see my mother.

Slowly, I made the connections and realized *that* was the reason Eileen never made those return visits—and the reason for the whispered conversations. Although it was several years before I heard anything more about Eileen and her new husband, I also never heard a negative word ever spoken about her. I think mostly there was a feeling of concern for her—that, perhaps, loneliness and fear of the future had made her vulnerable.

Eventually, Eileen and her husband—now with four kids: Mary Anne and three younger children—moved to Delaware, where they ran a campground. My mother had retired and moved to Florida. I don't know how it came to be that the two women reconnected, but every summer, my mother would drive from Florida to Delaware to help Eileen in the campground store. I remember that's where my mother was in July 1979 when I called to tell her our first baby, Zachary Thomas, was born.

My mother and Eileen not only reconnected, they shared an impressively strong friendship, always displaying great concern and love for one another. When they weren't together, they stayed in regular contact. One of them always called the other on January 19, the day of the tugboat accident, the day that changed both of their lives dramatically. I don't know how they handled birthday calls to one another: Eileen's birthday is March 28; my mother's, March 29. In later years, when my mother had heart surgery, Eileen went to Florida to care for her, staying for a month.

After 26 years of marriage, Eileen's second husband died a slow, painful death, bringing to an end a seriously troubled marriage.

In time, Eileen began dating again—someone she'd known for quite a while. One of Eileen's four sisters, Joanie, had passed away over 10 years earlier. Joanie's widower, Billy, and Eileen found some shared joy in dancing, simply being together, and being together with their adult children. When they made plans to marry, Eileen and Billy visited my mother in Florida and the three shared the happiness. Of course, Billy knew my brother Albie: They had once been brothers-in-law.

I had an odd feeling of comfort knowing that Eileen was with someone who knew my brother. I was thrilled when they married. Billy was aware, of course, of Eileen's painful past. Before they were married, he had a complete physical and his doctor said he was in good health. But just about six weeks later, Billy had a massive stroke and died. I remember my mother calling with that dreadful news. We were all terribly worried about Eileen.

It took time, but, little by little—with the help of her faith, her family, and friends—Eileen returned to the woman I knew her to be: the woman with the generous, loving heart who was hopeful and trusting.

A couple of years later, she met a kind, gentle man who attended her church. They married, but less than two years later, he died of leukemia. She was not yet 60 and widowed four times.

Years later, she had a friend, a nice man who traveled frequently to Germany on business. When my mother turned 80, we kids all chipped in, and my mother traveled with Eileen and her friend to Germany. The two women had shared so much, and now they would share my mother's first trip abroad. It was a wonderful, memorable time for my mother.

A couple of months later, Eileen's friend returned to Germany on business—this time alone. While there, he died of a heart attack.

In the fall of 2002, my sister Liz underwent surgery in Florida to have a cancerous tumor removed from her spine. The operation was long and intense. Liz expected to see me when she came out of recovery. It was comforting to see Michael arrive. Eileen came to the hospital, too. Liz had been through a terribly painful ordeal leading up to the surgery and still had a difficult time ahead. In her groggy state, she saw Eileen at her bedside and said lovingly, "Eileen, I knew you'd be here."

When Liz died, the plan was that she'd be buried with my mother, father, and brother. We had to determine exactly where her casket would be placed in the burial site. We did that, taking into consideration Eileen's long-time wish to be buried with her first husband, my brother Albie.

Several years ago, I was in a Bible study group with congregants from the Cutchogue Presbyterian Church, the Reformed Synagogue, and my church group, the North Fork Unitarian Universalist Fellowship. Retired Presbyterian minister Reverend Dick Ploth co-led the group with a young woman who was the intern rabbi for the synagogue at the time. One of the stories that made an impression on me was that of Ruth and Naomi.

After the death of Naomi's husband and two sons, she's left to care for herself, as well as her two daughters-in-law. That was not a good situation for women to find themselves in, in those days. Naomi had to leave her own people when she married her now deceased husband. Now she decides she's going to return to her people. She tells the daughters-in-law to do the same: "You're still young enough to give someone children," she told them. "May God look kindly on you and hope that's what happens."

Naomi knows that no one is going to take in three women, and she knows that if she goes with her daughters-in-law, life will be difficult for all three of them. Naomi has nothing to offer others in exchange for her food and security.

One daughter-in-law, Orpay, heeds Naomi's advice. She says her goodbyes and heads off. The other daughter-in-law, Ruth, "clung to her."

Do not press me to leave you or to turn back from following you! Where you go, I will go; where you lodge, I will lodge; your people shall be my people, and your God, my God. Where you die, I will die—there will I be buried. May the LORD do thus and so to me, and more as well, if even death parts me from you!

When Naomi saw that Ruth was determined to go with her, she said no more.

I heard that story and thought of my mother and Eileen's story.

Eileen still lives in Delaware. No one's been able to convince her yet to own a computer and try e-mail. We stay in touch with occasional phone conversations. It's a rare, special occasion that we see each other in person. In my mother's later years, she wrote Eileen a note in which she said, "Eileen, you have been my gift from Albie."

When I think of the place Eileen has in my family—and in my heart—I think about the words often spoken at weddings: "What God has joined together, let no man put asunder." I once heard someone say: "What God has joined together, no man *can* put asunder."

It was only a short time that my mother and Eileen were related as mother-in-law and daughter-in-law. For a much longer time, they enjoyed a close friendship, one that seemed to nourish them both.

I have a collage of pictures of my close friends with this quote from Katherine Mansfield: "The truth is, friendship is every bit as sacred and eternal as marriage." My mother and Eileen were good buddies and trusted confidants. It was a friendship that appeared to have all the components of a deep, lasting relationship—shared experiences, forgiveness, loyalty, love, and laughter.

I've talked with Eileen about her relationship with my mother. She ended our conversation saying, "We had a lot of laughs."

I'm glad it's what comes to her mind, but it's not what I would have expected to hear. It made me think of the words Barbra Streisand sang in the song, "The Way We Were":

> *What's too painful to remember*
> *We simply choose to forget*
> *So it's the laughter*
> *We will remember.*

Life turned upside down for Eileen and my mother—horribly, at times. They survived, independently and together. I believe time, love, and laughter were potent factors that enabled their relationship to endure and flourish. I'm grateful for their example—and for the joy they shared.

May 2010

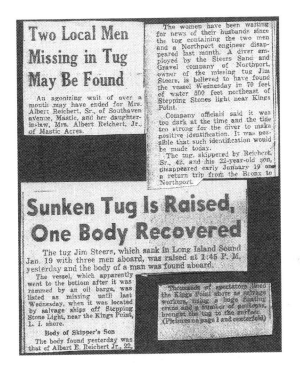

Two Local Men Missing in Tug May Be Found

An agonizing wait of over a month may have ended for Mrs. Albert Reichert, Sr., of Southaven avenue, Mastic, and her daughter-in-law, Mrs. Albert Reichert, Jr., of Mastic Acres.

The women have been waiting for news of their husbands since the tug containing the two men and a Northport engineer disappeared last month. A diver employed by the Steers Sand and Gravel company of Northport, owner of the missing tug Jim Steers, is believed to have found the vessel Wednesday in 70 feet of water 500 feet northeast of Stepping Stones light near Kings Point.

Company officials said it was too dark at the time and the tide too strong for the diver to make positive identification. It was possible that such identification would be made today.

The tug, skippered by Reichert, Sr., 42, and his 22-year-old son, disappeared early January 19 on a return trip from the Bronx to Northport.

Sunken Tug Is Raised, One Body Recovered

The tug Jim Steers, which sank in Long Island Sound Jan. 19 with three men aboard, was raised at 1:45 P. M. yesterday and the body of a man was found aboard.

The vessel, which apparently went to the bottom after it was rammed by an oil barge, was listed as missing until last Wednesday, when it was located by salvage ships off Stepping Stone Light, near the Kings Point, L. I. shore.

Body of Skipper's Son

The body found yesterday was that of Albert E. Reichert Jr., 22,

Thousands of spectators lined the Kings Point shore as salvage workers, using a huge floating crane and a number of pontoons, brought the tug to the surface. (Pictures on page 1 and centerfold.)

Winter 1958

My mother and Eileen Summer 1997

"Many people have asked me why there are three pedals in these grand pianos. Well, the pedal in the middle is there to separate the two other pedals."

—Victor Borge

The Perpetual Piano Student

If something has even a speck of sentimental value, I tend to have trouble tossing it out or giving it away. Clearing out becomes a slow process, but I stay determined to keep trying.

In my most recent attempt to lessen the amount of treasured keepers, I came across one of my old piano books for beginner students called, *Very First Classics*. It has 13 simple pieces by Beethoven, Brahms, Chopin, Mendelssohn, Tchaikovsky, and others. Its copyright date is 1957. The book of 13 classics cost 65 cents and was clearly meant for the new, young student. The pieces are arranged simply with rather large, easy-to-read notes.

I was 10 years old when I started taking piano lessons. I would have guessed that I was closer to 12, but, in addition to the music book, I found the program from my first recital, dated Sunday, April 27, 1958. My name appears at the top of the program, since I was the newest student and, thus, the first to perform.

I was such a shy, insecure child that I couldn't even speak my name clearly. I would say "Mary Ellen" in a barely audible mumble. People would call me "Maryanne," "Marion," and other first names that started with "M" and were a few syllables long.

It was terrifying to be the student to start Mrs. Phurst's recital—or, as the program reads, "A Musicale ~ Given by the Primary and Intermediate Piano Classes."

My friend Marilyn was also in the recital. We were both seated in the front right section of the living room, which doubled as the studio, but she was a few rows behind me. Marilyn was two years older than me and was a strong intermediate student. Of the 15 players that day, she was number 11.

I found a second recital program. This one, dated Sunday, March 8, 1959, was for the "Primary Pupils of Piano and Voice." This time, of the 19 student performers, I appear 12th on the program. My younger sister Liz was now a student, too. Her part in the recital was a little before mine. Marilyn was in a different recital, one for the more advanced students.

I have no recollection of playing at the recitals. I only remember the scary wait for my turn and what followed: the reception—with cookies. I didn't know it at the time, but those cookies were available at most bakeries. I'd never seen or tasted anything like them. When we had cookies, they were usually ordinary, like plain vanilla wafers. But here the table had sprawling trays of cookies in different shapes with dollops of chocolate, jelly fillings, and colorful sprinkles.

I soon forgot the anguish of the recital. The cookies were incredibly delicious, and there were so many of them. I remember following the lead of another student, and filling my pockets with as many cookies as I dared to take home.

My mother didn't attend the recitals. When the teacher talked with her about attending, she said it was hard for her to get out with all of the other kids at home. If my mother had attended, I'm sure that she would have given me a stern lesson in recital etiquette.

Mrs. Phurst lived near enough so that when my mother was out doing errands, bringing me to my lesson was convenient. I could also ride my bike, or walk. I liked learning to play the piano and wish that I had been able to stay with it, but I was scared off. At one of my lessons, Mrs. Phurst was coughing. She coughed hard and persistently and finally left the room quickly. It seemed like a long wait before she came back. When she did, she reeked of alcohol. Another time, she was so drunk that she could barely talk. I had experienced my father's occasional drunkenness and hated it. Although I was frightened, somehow I sat through the lesson, and then ran the whole way home.

After just about two years, that was my last lesson with Mrs. Phurst. I'm sure there were other piano teachers somewhere nearby, but getting to lessons anywhere else likely would have added to my mother's burdensome days. As a young widow, she had more than enough to do. It would be decades before I took another piano lesson.

I'm not sure where my mother got the piano that we had. It was a used upright. She played—and quite beautifully. I'll never reach her level of playing and that's OK with me. I just hope to keep playing the piano, a little or a lot, at any skill level.

I started lessons again once my three kids began taking them. But, for one reason or another, I stopped. Time would pass, and I'd give it another try and another and another and so on and so on. Throughout my adult years—with five different, good teachers—I've attempted unsuccessfully to stick with lessons. Now with my sixth piano teacher, I think it's going to work. For one thing, I can take a lesson every other week, and that works for me. And now, my perspective on what's important in life has influenced my commitment to playing.

Over the years, as my kids were growing up, we had some clunky pianos, but we were happy just to have a piano in the house. What we have now is a beautiful Kawai grand piano. The woman who sold it to us said she just wasn't playing it enough to keep it. Later, after we learned it was the last big gift her husband had bought her before he died, I made a point of letting her know, in writing, that we treasured the piano and would take good care of it.

I just want to sit at it and make a little music. So far, that's what I'm doing. I still don't set aside enough practice time, so my progress is slow. To get anywhere in our house you have to walk by the piano, and I often feel a tug to pause and sit at it. But many things tug at my time. I love when I surrender to the urge to play, even if it's for just five minutes. That's certainly not quality practice time, but, at the end of the day, I feel better knowing that my hands have touched piano keys.

I don't worry anymore about how my redundant practicing sounds to my husband. Rather, I wish he were doing the same with his guitar, banjo, or the piano. The joy of music and the value of playing an instrument is something that we share and have tried to pass along to our kids.

At 18 months old, our granddaughter has a strong response to music, which I think all kids have when they're encouraged to experience it. And she charms the whole family with her dancing. We hope to help sustain her delight in all things musical.

I continue to let go and clear out, but I'm keeping that 65-cent book of classics. I love turning to the first piece in the book and remembering "To a Wild Rose." I enjoy both classic and contemporary pieces. In a couple of weeks, I'll travel across the country to visit a dear friend in Oregon. Sue was my college roommate. We try to see each other once a year. We'll go to the Saturday Market in Portland, which is now a Saturday *and* Sunday event. Roads close, and vendors sell a wide array of goods.

I'll pack my piano music to practice on her husband's electric keyboard. I've been playing a simple piece called "Come Saturday Morning." It's from the old movie *The Sterile Cuckoo*. The words are:

Come Saturday morning, I'm going away with my friend.
We'll Saturday-spend till the end of the day, just I and my friend.
We'll travel for miles in our Saturday smiles, and then we'll move on.
But we will remember long after Saturday's gone.

When I play "Come Saturday Morning" at home, I think of my friend. Sometimes it's a sentimental connection that influences the pieces that I decide to work on. That's been so with other pieces like "The Rose," "Somewhere Out There," "Sunrise, Sunset," and others. When I'm looking at things to let go of and clear out, if I'm looking at the piano music, I probably won't get far at all.

I'm aware of having a life that's blessed in many ways. In the big picture of one's health, it's minor, but it pleases me to note that I have all 10 of my fingers in working order. They're getting a little bumpy and sometimes grow sore by the joints, but they're OK. They can do all sorts of neat things, including play a simple little piano tune.

September 2010

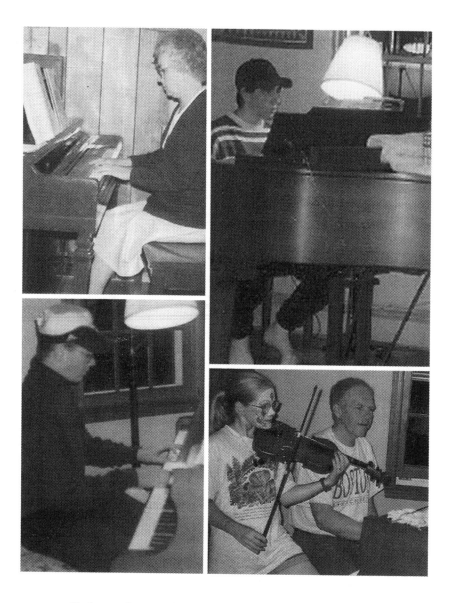

Clockwise, from top left: My mother on one of our old pianos;
Zac; face-painted Kim on violin, accompanied by Tom; Jeremy

SUNDAY, APRIL 27th, 1958, at 3:00 P. M.

☆

Musicale Given by the Primary and Intermediate Piano Classes
with Joan Danowski, Soprano

☆

PROGRAM

1. CHASING BUTTERFLIES   2. SINGING
Mary Ellen Reichert

1. IN THE ORCHARD   2. BUGLES
Karen Hallock

1. MY PONY   2. WEATHER SONG
Brenda Masterson

1. SLEEP BABY SLEEP   2. SAILBOAT
Susan Adipietro

1. HALLOWE'EN PUMPKIN   2. SEE THE PONY
Carol Schubert

1. THE BELLS   2. MAY DANCE
Paulette D'Amato

1. SQUIRRELS   2. SAILING SHIP
Ruth Tank

THE WHITE SWAN OF SAMARKAND .... Alberti
LOCH LOMOND .... Scotch
VIENNESE WALTZ .... Charles
Miss Danowski

WALTZ .... Schubert
SHORT'NIN' BREAD .... American Folk
Valerie Krzemien

MYSTIC NIGHT .... Kitcher
SLIDING ON ICE .... Gurlitt
Trudy Froelich

CRADLE SONG .... Mozart
WHISTLING BOY .... Diller
Marilyn Adipietro

WALTZ .... Moravian
STAR OF THE SEA .... French Folk
Jacqueline Doyen

BY THE RIVERSIDE .... Hopson
DONKEY SERENADE .... Friml
Anita Monticella

DANCING DOLL .... Kanschau
PATTER OF THE RAIN .... Kanschau
THE ASH GROVE .... Welsh Folk
Renee Salzman

RHODESIAN SKETCHES .... Bell
     1. SONG OF THE FIVE STAMP MILL
     2. WOODPECKER
     3. THE LAZY LION
     4. BUNDU LULLABY
     5. AFTER A SHOWER OF RAIN
     6. THE LITTLE BLUE BUCK
     7. MOSQUITO
     8. FLYING ANT
     9. DOVE
     *10. PICCANIN'S DANCE
     *11. THE CHATTERING PUCCANYANI
Dorothy Muller

* Duets with Mrs. Frederick Muller.

MUSICALE

Given by

PRIMARY PUPILS OF PIANO AND VOICE

with

SHIRLEY DURHAM, SENIOR PIANO STUDENT

Sunday, March 8th, 1959, at 3:00 P. M.

☆

PROGRAM

1. TROT AWAY   2. SINGING
Joyce Potokin

1. DRUMMER BOY   2. WESTMINSTER CHIMES
Elijah Green

1. IN THE ORCHARD   2. SAILBOAT
Barbara Kwasnik

1. JUMPING JACK   2. FAIRYLAND
Mark Kwasnik

1. HALLOWEEN PUMPKIN   2. BUGLES
Diane Alas

1. SLEEP BABY SLEEP   2. GOING SWIMMING
Annette Davis

1. MY PONY   2. WEATHER SONG
Wallace Matteson

1. O HOW BEAUTIFUL   2. THE DOVES
Kathleen Sewell

1. LITTLE LAMB   2. RING OUT WILD BELLS
Pamela Carozza

1. IN MY LITTLE BOAT   2. RAIN, RAIN GO TO SPAIN
Elizabeth Reichert

1. DANCE   2. SAILING
Kathleen Kelmer

1. BURNEY BEE   2. THE NIGHTINGALE
Mary Ellen Reichert

LULLABY .... BRAHMS
BY THE BEND OF THE RIVER .... CLARA EDWARDS
Susan Morrison

SKIP TO M'LOU .... KENTUCKY MOUNTAIN TUNE
THE SILENT PIG ....AN
Eugenia Van Names

THINKING CAP .... SCHUBERT
THE SHEPHERDESS .... FRENCH FOLK SONG
Gladys Rech

SNOW DANCE .... MOZART
THE COWSLIP BELL .... 17th CENTURY ENGLISH
Carol Schubert

SKATING LADY .... FROST
THE YO-YO .... WILLIAMS
Susan Adipietro

THE BUSY MILL WHEEL .... JESSE
THE RIDE OF THE SPACE MEN .... CURCIO
Brenda Matteson

WEDDING DAY AT TROLDHAUGEN .... GREIG
Shirley Durham

"The final forming of a person's character lies in their own hands."
—*Anne Frank*

Careful With That Glass, Things Can Break

We had a small Easter dinner with our son, Zac; his wife, Michelle; and their daughter, Madison. We felt the need for a small, quiet holiday. I made ham with raisin sauce, grilled sweet potatoes and carrots, sautéed asparagus, and mashed potatoes. As a matter of tradition, we had Polish kielbasa, pungent horseradish sauce, and an outstandingly delicious babka from a bakery in Jamesport.

I like setting the table for a special dinner. I don't have "everyday" dishes and "good" dishes. I have "everyday" dishes and "different everyday" dishes. But I enjoy fixing the table with cloth napkins, candles, flowers, and stemmed glassware. The stemmed glasses are technically wine glasses, but I like having any kind of drink in an attractive stemmed glass.

It doesn't matter what the container is, when I ask my husband, Tom, if he'd like some water, he used to respond, "I never touch the stuff."

But he has since learned that drinking a good amount of water every day has definite health benefits. When Tom had his gall bladder removed, the doctor checked his pancreas and expressed concern about its texture. The doctor has suggested that Tom watch his alcohol intake. He has opted to refrain altogether.

I enjoy wine, but after Tom stopped drinking, I decided to not drink in front of him. My abstinence proved unnecessary: In general, Tom is not a risk-taker, and he wants to live a healthy life, so for him, dropping alcohol from his diet was a matter of common sense, not great sacrifice.

I enjoy both red and white wine, something smooth and not too sweet. I like the way white wine tastes with the fresh vegetables that we were having for that Easter dinner, although I think that my favorite combination is a chilled chardonnay with a savory salmon dinner. There's just something about those two particular flavors that make me say, "Hmm," with almost every bite.

I didn't drink alcohol when I was pregnant with our three kids or during the several months of nursing that followed, and I don't recall missing it at all.

There have been times when I've had some bad experiences with wine. When I didn't stop after a couple of glasses, I've embarrassed myself, saying or doing something that I later—or immediately—regretted.

Alcohol has been no dear friend to my close or distant relatives. Alcoholism is a part of our family history. I didn't know my father very well or for very long—he died when I was 10—but I know that when he drank, it wasn't a matter of sipping wine with dinner.

When our family moved from Queens, New York, to eastern Long Island, some of my older siblings were teenagers. I asked one if moving was difficult at an age when friends are so important. The firm response: "No way. I was relieved. I couldn't wait to go." That response had to do with the memory of friends witnessing my father falling, drunk, on our front walkway. Even if it happened just once, once was enough to look forward to starting over with new friends.

I didn't have that kind of experience. I was younger, and it wasn't until after we moved, when I was seven, that I had friends come to our house. I didn't ask my sibling if any new friends ever saw my father drunk—*my* new friends did, but they didn't know it.

My younger sister, Liz, and I and two of our friends, Marilyn and her younger sister, Susan were playing in our living room one day when my father came home from his job as a tugboat captain. He worked on the tugboat for stretches of a week or two at a time. This day, while my mother fixed dinner in the kitchen, my father came into the living room and sat in a cushioned chair with his feet on an ottoman. He joked with us and was generally rather merry and playful. If I got close to where he sat, my father reached out to tickle me. Such playfulness was totally out of character for him.

"Your father's so funny," Marilyn said.

I didn't think he was funny at all because I knew he was drunk. My relationship with him was not playful, and it was not fun. It was tense, distant, and cold. That's what I knew. That's what I had learned to live with. I didn't know the guy who was trying to be funny, and I didn't trust him. I didn't know how to respond to him.

It was clear that my mother wasn't comfortable either. She called me into the kitchen and said, "Take your friends to your room."

We played for a while in the bedroom I shared with my sisters and then left to go to our friends' house. As we walked through the house to leave, we didn't see or hear my father. He had probably fallen asleep.

Across the narrow dirt road at Marilyn and Susan's house, both parents were home, just like at my house. We walked in the back door and through the kitchen. Just like at my house, my friends' father was in the living room. He was sitting at the piano, playing without reading music, when he heard us walk in. He turned toward us just briefly and gave us a shy, but friendly, smile.

I'm convinced my father loved all of his kids. He just had great difficulty showing it. To say that he was unapproachable is an understatement. Over the years, I've imagined him as an old man, as a gentler father, and a loving, fun grandfather. I don't imagine a man drinking irresponsibly. In my imagination—my fantasy—he worked out whatever issues had caused him to drink. I imagine helping him put his jacket around his shoulders when he's chilly. I imagine an old man whom I could touch lovingly.

I remember Dean Martin, a singer from my parents' generation, whom many considered handsome and talented. As part of his TV act, he would often sing with a drink in his hand and appear to be inebriated. The audience considered it funny. I never understood why.

Drunkenness scared me then, and it still makes me uncomfortable. Lots of people claim they can hold their alcohol just fine, no matter how much they drink. That's what they think.

At many formal events, alcohol flows generously and plentifully. Often, all you have to do is catch a waiter's eye and signal for another round of drinks. It's an arrangement that fosters heavy, thoughtless drinking. Catch an eye. Wave a hand. Have another drink—and another and another, again and again.

I often think of a friend who once had a serious drinking problem. He said that one afternoon his wife made one small, but poignant, comment about his drinking. Her comment stunned and offended— and also motivated—him. That afternoon, he vowed to himself that he would never drink again. It was New Year's Eve, and he worked as a bartender that night, pouring countless drinks, but not one for himself—that night or any other. His story impressed me when he first shared it, and I continue to be in awe of his strength and discipline.

In Massachusetts in the summer 2009, a racially charged confrontation between a black Harvard University professor and a white police sergeant escalated and became national news. President Barack Obama got involved, hoping to insert some calm into the volatile situation. He invited the professor and the police officer to the White House to sit together and talk over a beer.

The men sat outside in the Rose Garden with the President, as well as Vice-President Joe Biden. The media covered the story in great detail, making quite a fuss about the kind of beer each man drank. The media made much too little over the fact that Vice-President Biden didn't drink a beer that day—and never does.

He grew up around close family members and neighbors who were alcoholics. That affected him so adversely that he never drinks alcohol. I think Biden's strong response to the destructive drinking he witnessed growing up would have been an important news story. But, for the most part, the media neglected to tell it.

I want to drink the way that I like to eat: aware. Aware of what I'm taking in and how much. When our daughter, Kim, visits, she invites us to share in a blessing before we eat. She often chooses words about being intentional, being grateful, and being aware of the source of our food, the hands that prepare it, and the nourishment it provides. There is a respectful nature to eating with intention that can work with drinking, too. We end up doing both a little slower.

One night when our kids were all still living at home, my in-laws joined us for dinner. My father-in-law remarked, "You eat to socialize. We eat to get full." His style of eating was probably set in his younger years, when he'd come in from his farm to fill his belly and then get back out to work again before dark.

My father-in-law was right: Our style is different from his. For one thing, Tom and I used to say to our kids, "Don't eat until the cook sits." Translated, that meant don't put fork to mouth until mom is sitting, too.

My mother never let us kids take telephone calls during dinnertime. With our kids, we shut off the phone and set a timer for 20 minutes. Even if they chose to gobble their food hurriedly, they still had to sit at the table until the timer went off. During that time, we asked them to tell us something about their day. At first, Jeremy, our quiet middle child, resented this request. His two loquacious siblings had no trouble adding his time to theirs, but it wasn't long before he claimed his fair share of time and would firmly let an interrupter know, "I'm not finished telling."

So, yes, we saw dinnertime as a time for more than just getting full. We wanted intentional time for nourishment, both physical and emotional. During those early parenting years, we never had alcohol with our dinners, at least not during the week. Our dinnertimes were far from perfect, but they set examples about one thing or another.

And now, when no one impressionable is watching, I still want to be careful and intentional with my choices. When my jaw feels tight at the end of the day, sometimes I think about having a glass of wine. That's fine, but I want to be aware of my alternatives. I also enjoy the comfort of having a cup of flavorful hot tea. I have a pottery mug that's as soothing to hold as the tea is to sip. When I fill it with one of my favorite teas, I have that same chardonnay-and-salmon experience that makes me say, "Hmm," with each sip. Nowadays, I don't need to worry much about being a poor role model, unless, of course, I slurp my tea with way too much gusto.

At our Easter dinner, two-year-old Madison raised her sippy cup full of organic apple juice and proclaimed, "Cheers." Carefully, we all clinked our glasses together. She knows you have to be careful with glasses.

On my face, I had a smile. In my head and in my heart, I had a hope and a prayer. I want my kids and their kids to have good times with people they enjoy. I hope they have many occasions to raise glasses in fellowship with others. It's been done for centuries—with and without alcohol—as a symbol of togetherness. It's a way of expressing a feeling of unity with others, with the sentiment spoken in a toast or in a blessing. It can also just be a way to say, "We're here. We're together."

In a short time, sippy cups are put away. Other glasses of one kind or another replace them. Other drinks, oftentimes alcoholic, replace apple juice. That doesn't have to be a bad thing. It requires care—care about how we drink, when we drink, and why.

It requires being responsible.

Otherwise, something could get broken. Handled clumsily, pretty stemmed glasses, beer mugs, or even shot glasses can break. But there are things far more important and more fragile than any glass. There are the promises that we have made to ourselves and to others, our treasured relationships, and impressionable children.

So to the drinkers at casual family gatherings, holiday dinners, big parties—and to those who drink in the quiet of their homes—I say, let's be careful. Let's watch out for all those things that are breakable. Cheers.

June 2011

> *"Under certain circumstances,*
> *profanity provides a relief denied even to prayer."*
> —*Mark Twain*

From One Mouth to Another Ear

Usually I can put clothes in the dryer without any trouble. But I was hurrying—not a good way to move through a day. I like what Henry David Thoreau said: "Nothing can be more useful to a man than a determination not to be hurried." It's not just a matter of "haste makes waste." I believe what I've read from spiritual writers: It's an obstacle to our spiritual growth. When I hurry, I feel lucky if I have only a minor mishap.

I was almost finished tossing clothes in the dryer. I groaned when a wet brown sock fell right next to the cat's litter box, landing on the floor on top of litter that the cat had kicked out of the box. I stretched awkwardly, reaching and bending, rushing to get it, and hit my head on the corner of a metal shelf as I stood up. Loud and clear, I said, "Shit."

The pain didn't linger. I recovered quickly, set the dryer, and went into the kitchen where my husband, Tom, sat at the counter.

"Are you okay?" he asked.

"Yeah." I told him what had happened. "You know, my response in there was spontaneous. Yet, I know that if Madison" —our two-year-old granddaughter— "was near enough to hear, I wouldn't have cursed."

"Or if anyone else was near enough," Tom added.

"Well, I'm not so sure about that." My self-editing tool can kick-start rather quickly, but around some friends, I can easily forget that I have such a tool.

I've known Tom for about 40 years, and during that time, I have heard him say "shit," I think, maybe twice. I've heard him say—let's use the word "farkleberry"—only when we watch a movie and I say, "I missed that. What'd that guy say?"

We had some work done in the house recently and had to sleep upstairs in the guest room. I like having something—a bench or a chest—at the foot of the bed to catch a tossed blanket or to keep an extra one handy. There's nothing like that at the foot of the guest bed, so I found an old wood board and set it on smaller pieces of wood as if it were a bench and put it along the end of the bed. I forgot to mention it to Tom.

He got up during the night, walked barefoot in the dark, and slammed his foot into a corner of my new end-of-bed bench. I awoke when I heard Tom's foot meet the wood and he groaned. That would have been a perfect opportunity to release a long list of curse words. If he did, he kept it to himself. The toenails on that foot stayed purple for months.

It's not that I'm intentionally testing Tom. Profanity just doesn't seem to surface when he's angry, frustrated, injured, or just trying to make a strong point. Maybe it's about personal style, maybe habit.

Our combined families consist of a wide range of education levels and professions, as well as a colorful variety of personalities. I'd bet anything that some of our family members use profanity, but I've never heard it. It likely depends on where they are and whom they're with.

I've heard that cursing can be a good stress reliever. I would say that my mother used words to relieve her stress rather often, though never using "farkleberry." She had her favorites, which I won't list here.

My mother was a big New York Mets fan and liked watching the games on TV. During one of her visits with us from Florida, the house was empty except for the two of us. She watched a ballgame on TV while I was busy in other rooms. Each time I walked by and saw her looking relaxed, enjoying an all-American pastime, I thought, "This is great. She really enjoys the games. I love seeing her relaxed." Then she startled me when she stood up, walked out of the room, and said in a dismissive tone, "Jackasses."

I wasn't sure what had happened: A bad call? A fight? "What happened, Ma?"

"They're losing," she answered, matter-of-factly.

I guess that's how sports fans are. I liked that my mother was a baseball fan, but I hadn't realized that her team support could provoke anger. And maybe it wasn't really anger. Maybe it was just a habit, a way of talking that sounded like anger. Whatever the case, that was Mom, the Mets fan whom I knew and loved.

As a young widow with lots of kids, my mother was also apt to pray aloud. If I were arguing with my sisters over whose turn it was to set the table, my mother would interrupt with an earnest plea to the Divine: "Jesus, Mary, and Joseph! Somebody just set the table." In her later years, my mother was more discerning about how she used religious words.

While our three kids were all still in school, Tom and I hosted an exchange student from Paraguay. One Sunday night, Tom's parents joined us for dinner. Tom and his parents conversed at one end of the table. At the other end, where all the kids sat, I heard our student guest ask, "What does it mean, 'peez me ov'? I hear all the time. 'Don't peez me ov,' 'You peez me ov.'"

The response he received surprised me. Our son—I think it was Zac—told him to shush, to lower his voice. He shot a quick glance in his grandparents' direction.

I considered alleviating concerns by saying, "It's really OK. I'm sure they'll think it's funny," but I let it be, amused by the respectful protection our children gave the grandparents, even though I knew it wasn't necessary.

A relative who was close to retiring as a public high school English teacher once shared with me her dismay about her school environment: "I still love my work," she said. "When I close my door I'm totally involved and happy. But when I walk through the hallways, I often feel that all of my senses are being assaulted."

That's how it is in some places.

It was quite different when I was a high school student at a parochial school. Except for a few nuns whose anger was out of control, the environment was orderly and respectful. Back in 1965, we used typewriters, not computers. We had special round erasers with little brushes attached to fix errors. I was a good typist—fast and accurate—but, this day, I made more mistakes than usual.

Sister Tomasina's class reflected her good teaching style and pleasant manner, so there was no need to let mistakes upset me. But stopping to fix yet another error frustrated me. Annoyed, I said, "Oh for cryin' out loud." But I only spoke half of it in a way that could be heard, leaving the rest spoken in my head. So what came out was, "Oh, for c..." It didn't occur to me that what I said sounded like, "Oh, farkleberry." Sharon —a sweet, reticent girl who I liked and who sat across from me—looked at me and said nothing, except, "Mary Ellen." Her tone and her facial expression translated to "I am shocked and disappointed."

"What?" I asked her and, shamelessly, went on erasing and brushing.

Had I actually said, "For cryin' out loud," that would have gone unnoticed. A good, strong "darn it" would have been inconsequential. Even a soft-spoken "damn" wouldn't have caused trouble. But hearing farkleberry in a setting where every class started with a prayer—was too much.

I recalled all of this recently as I said those very same words—"Oh for cryin' out loud"—in that same trailing-off, unfinished way. But this time, I heard it. I heard what it had sounded like to Sharon. It was a way overdue "ah-ha" moment.

I've noticed that I tend to curse when I'm annoyed with myself. I was writing with a deadline recently and had just made a fresh pot of coffee. Tom sat in another room with his own project. Instead of calling to him, "The coffee's ready," I fixed him a cup and then brought it to him, hurriedly. When I noticed that, in my haste, I had left a trail of spills, I greeted Tom, coffee in hand, with "Shit," and then I added, "Oh, perfect. Now I'll get back to writing about profanity."

For me, it's a spiritual matter, in a broad sense. I wasn't coming from the place where I am most comfortable, the place where I feel truly present. Had I been in that place while fixing the coffee, I would have acknowledged the nudging that I was getting: Either get coffee and move back to the computer, or bring Tom coffee, too. And, in either case, relax and breathe. There will be enough time.

Instead, I moved quickly. I spilled. I cursed.

I spill other times, and I don't curse. Spills happen. It wasn't the spill that had caused my reaction. It was moving in one direction while my head was in another. My not bringing Tom the coffee would have been more of an act of kindness to both of us.

One summer, my dear friend Maureen and I shared a long weekend in a rural part of Colorado. We attended a dinner party that a mutual friend hosted on the spacious deck of her mountain-view home. Our friend had neighbors, but their homes weren't visible. Humming birds stayed busy at the feeders hanging on the deck. A cat sat on a window ledge inside the house and watched the birds with relaxed resignation. The temperature was perfect. A gentle breeze encouraged the wind chimes to play a soothing tune. The setting urged guests gently to sigh, converse, and be comfortable. I was there, present and willing to oblige.

Another guest, an attractive, rather talkative, middle-aged woman, said "farkleberry" in every other sentence. After a while, I didn't hear anything else that she said, just "farkleberry farkleberry farkleberry, farkleberry, farkleberry." I felt as though I was listening to someone scratching a fingernail on a chalkboard. When the conversation turned to a piece of pottery that a local artist had created, the woman said, "It is so farkleberry beautiful."

I had the image of this one-of-a-kind, handmade bowl, with its exquisite colors, feeling all puffed up with pride as we gave it our adoring attention. And then, I imagined it dumbfounded and deflated, wondering with some confusion, "What? I'm *what* kind of beautiful?" The woman's manner of speaking went from distracting to absurd.

I don't believe that refraining from profanity makes one morally superior. I know a few people who wouldn't dream of cursing in any manner but who have some values that I wouldn't want my grandkids embracing. The opposite is also true: Some people who say "farkleberry" in certain settings make me uncomfortable, but they are, otherwise, people whom I would hold up as role models.

I have noticed that when people burp they say, "Excuse me." Not so when they say "farkleberry." I wonder about that. Sometimes I'd rather hear a burp.

I do think that the shock value of strong profanity is weakening. That's not good news to me. If the "F bomb" is defused, surely something else will take its place, maybe something worse to hear. Or maybe a different word, something lovely and innocent will be hijacked and distorted. And what if the new profanity is worse?

Or what if it could be a word like "lavender"? "Lavender" is definitely a favorite of mine. Besides liking lavender, the flower, for its looks and scent, I like the way the word sounds. While I walked from church to my car recently, some children playing outside showed me their fresh-snipped bouquets of lavender. We shared our admiration for it, and Julia, one of the young girls, said, "I think 'Lavender' would make a pretty name."

Hmm. Sweet thought.

But, if in desperation for a new word bomb, others took ownership of "lavender," how would I feel looking up at a highway overpass and seeing: "Lavender you."

Impossible. It would never happen: too many letters. It wouldn't be cost-effective. It is likely that the "F bomb" painters would go with something shorter.

"Giggle" is another word that I like. It's hard to say without feeling a smile starting. But it's probably still too long for concrete surfaces and other public places.

Maybe "bliss." That's a sweet word. Someone could have a grand time messing that one up.

But four-letter words seem preferable. "Love you" would fit—and it would have the shock effect.

Profanity isn't new. All sorts of people use it. Some of it is strong; some mild. Some profanity is delivered with emotion and some is just babbled out. I've used words that have had nothing to do with profanity but have hurt others deeply. I want to be more aware of the words that I use. I believe words have an impact that sets off a vibration. This poor earth—and all of us on it—need all the good vibrations we can get. When it comes to bombs, I don't like any kind. They all disturb the peace. I like lavender.

2011

"You are our living link to the past. Tell your grandchildren the story
of the struggles waged. . . . And tell them your own story as well—
because [everyone] has a story to tell."
—President George H.W. Bush,
State of the Union Address, 1990

Where's Dad?

"How does she do it?" I wonder as I watch her from my bedroom window. She gathers. She builds. She's efficient, practical, and patient. And, on top of all that, she can fly.

I've been watching a mama robin build a nest in the rhododendron bush. If I opened the bedroom window, I could practically touch it. She completed the gathering and building and then spent her time sitting. Mama Bird, all alone in the nest for hours on end. I found myself asking a question that's likely been asked countless times throughout history: Where's Dad?

I did a little reading and learned some things about robins' nesting behavior. Still, the words "Where's Dad?" stayed with me.

Dad's busy. He's in the military. He's in med school. He's in the White House. He's doing the dishes. He's doing time. He's cutting the church lawn. He's cutting unemployment benefits. He's checking the battery. He's checking out. He's listening. He's fighting. He's being fitted for a prosthesis. He's being fitted for a tux. Dad's around.

My father, Albert Henry Reichert, was 5'11". He had brown hair, brown eyes, a medium build and was quite handsome. He was the sixth of eight children in a Lutheran family. His father was stern and stingy. His mother, who died when he was a teenager, was a good, kind woman.

Robins are said to be among the last songbirds that we hear singing as evening sets in.

My father had a good singing voice and would sing to my mother when he walked her home after dates. He told her Frankie Laine's songs were in a good key for him to sing along. A couple of his favorites were "Someday" and "Lucky Old Sun."

My parents married in 1936. He was 19; she, 17 and pregnant. They were married in the Catholic Church, but because my father was non-Catholic, they were denied the tradition of standing on the altar. They stood just below it.

When female robins choose their mates, they normally base their preference on the males' songs, plumage, and territory quality. Robins are friendly birds.

My father was a guy who enjoyed good times with a loyal group of friends. Now, the immediacy of family responsibility clipped his wings early.

Once a female robin has selected a mate, the nest-building follows, with the female taking charge. Building a nest takes about five or six days. The nest is made of three layers: grasses, mud, and fine grasses. Yarn or a piece of plastic wrap might even show up in a nest.

In 1939, my parents lived in a fifth-floor walk-up in Washington Heights with two sons, Albie and John. They enjoyed their own space and the friendship of other young couples in their building. But when my father lost his job, my parents gave up the apartment and moved in with his father. It seemed like a good option.

Pop was widowed and still had two teenage daughters at home. My parents would have a secure place to live and could catch up financially. Maybe the teenage girls would benefit from the company.

Robins' typical nesting season is April through May. Robins lay about four eggs and incubate them for 12 to 14 days. They can have two or three broods in one season.

While still at Pop's house in 1940, my parents had a daughter, Anne, named for my mother. By this time, Pop's two youngest daughters had married and moved out. In 1942 and 1943, my parents had two more sons, Bobby and Billy. They still lived at Pop's.

At certain times of the year, male robins get together for the night in large communal roosts. In other words, the guy birds hang out together all night, even during the breeding period. They roost together at night but go back to their nests during the day.

In 1943, when our country was in the middle of World War II, my father was a rugged 27-year-old. Driven by patriotism and a desire to be part of the war action, I suppose, he attempted to enlist in the military. Perhaps he saw himself more valuable as an enlisted man than a family man. The military turned him down, either for having flat feet, five kids, or maybe some combination of reasons.

I guess that when a guy wants to stretch his wings and hang with a different flock for a while, he'll find a way: My father, undeterred by the Selective Service rejection, volunteered with the Merchant Marine.

In mid-October 1943, he wrote this first entry in the diary that he kept: "We left Frisco on the 7th of September. The trip was unusually long due to our backtracking to throw off an enemy sub. . . . I have been so busy upon arriving here that I have not had the time to write home. I miss Anne and the children immensely and hope that they are OK."

On that day that my father left the country, the oldest of his five kids was seven. The baby, five weeks old. The next oldest was 18 months old. Two little ones in diapers, cloth diapers fastened with big safety pins and rubber pants that fit over the diaper. My mother had no wet wipes for easy clean up. She washed everything and didn't have a washing machine. What is there not to be OK about?

On October 18, 1943, my father wrote in his diary from Australia: "Today I begin classes in navigation at Sydney College—it should prove interesting."

He wrote on October 30, "I have been seeing quite a lot of this town. Most everything is reasonable, including nightclubs. Lonesome for Anne and kiddies."

Earthworms are a favorite food of robins. They also eat caterpillars, beetles, and grasshoppers. Fruits and berries account for 60 percent of a robin's diet.

My father wrote in his diary on November 21, 1943: "We boarded a Dutch ship with 1,100 troops. . . . Conditions on board are terrible.

We have to sleep on deck, and only two meals are served—breakfast at 7 a.m. and dinner at 4. Food is served by army and is rotten."

"Three letters from Anne today," he wrote on December 22, 1943. "Love her with all my heart."

Two days later, he wrote, "Christmas Eve. Quite a few boys are drunk from drinking 'jungle juice.' I had invitation to join them but declined with thanks. Christmas is no time to be drunk. Expect to attend mass tomorrow."

Attending mass must have been my mother's influence. To my knowledge, my father never attended mass or any church service when he was home.

On December 30, my father lamented, "Still no mail. Felt blue because of it. John's birthday today. Wish I was with him."

"Another day without mail," my father wrote on December 31. "Last mail was the 22nd. What does the New Year hold in store for me? . . . Will make up to Anne in the coming year for all the heartaches I caused her. No more foolishness again. Just Anne and the children and I."

"No mail as usual again," he wrote on January 1, 1944:. "Hope the year 1944 will prove to be happier than '43. I'll do my best to make it so."

The next day, my father wrote, "Still no mail. Was paid today. Will send Anne $100 more. Only reason for continuing. . . . At the end . . . will be able to be independent. May buy own home."

On January 3, he wrote, "Went across the Bay to send money order. Anne will be pleased when she receives all the money orders." He followed up two days later, writing, "Received six letters from home. Everything is fine, except that Anne fell down the cellar."

On January 10, my father shared, "Received pleasant surprise. Instead of getting second mate, I was made Chief Officer."

"Like job immensely," he wrote the next day. "Doing same work I did home. Docking ships, placing derrick along side, etc."

On January 26, my father "received cable from Dr. to the [e]ffect of Anne's illness." He noted on February 8, "Received notification of seriousness of Anne's illness. Will be sent home." On March 25, he wrote, "Passing through Nevada—snow on mountaintops."

In 1947, another baby. I was born in the fall of that year. My mother said that she wanted to get my father "involved," so she planned a home birth.

Home was still my grandfather's house. By this time, my father was a tugboat captain with a week-on/week-off schedule. He missed the birth.

In 1949 and 1952, two more daughters, Liz and Patty, were born, in the hospital, like the first five.

During nesting season, robins carry mouthfuls of tasty worms to their babies. They will fill their mouth until you think nothing more could possibly fit, and still they continue to try to pick up more. In the process, robins drop stuff. Their beaks are full, still they try to pick up more.

One of my father's older sisters, Edna, died of cancer in 1950. Months later, her husband died in a horrific work-related accident in South Amboy, New Jersey. Over 400 tons of military explosives blew up under mysterious circumstances, killing 31 dockworkers and injuring hundreds. The dockworkers had been transferring military explosives and dynamite from railcars to a barge. My uncle's death left three daughters—Barbara, Edna, and Mary—orphaned.

None of my father's seven siblings felt they could take the girls. Relatives on their father's side took in Mary, the youngest. She was my age: 2. My parents took in the two older girls, Barbara, 10, who had special needs, and Edna, who was seven. My mother said it was my father's decision to bring the girls into our already crowded family. She said that he couldn't bear to see them go to an orphanage. They lived with us for seven years.

Thirteen of us—three adults and 10 kids—lived in my grandfather's three-bedroom house, along with our dog, Pal. My grandfather had his bedroom. My four brothers shared another, and the two cousins shared the last. My three sisters and I shared a bedroom that had once been the front porch. My parents slept in the living room on a pull-out couch, the kind where actors in TV commercials wore big smiles, showing us how easy it all was for a couch to become a bed. The 13 of us shared just one bathroom. Pal was the lucky one.

I know my mother wanted to have her own nest long before it became a reality. That January 2, 1944, diary entry—"May buy own home"—came to fruition in 1955.

I don't know how my parents came to find the quiet little town called Mastic. The house sat at the end of a long dirt road. I was seven and recall feeling good that our new home was made of brick. No big bad wolf could huff and puff and blow our house down. Oddly, we downsized to a two-bedroom house and still had just one bathroom. Quick renovations added two bedrooms and a second bathroom.

Male and female robins have calls and alarm notes. Only the male robin sings. Perhaps Mama bird—the nest-builder—just has no energy left for frivolity.

That wasn't always so with my mother. My parents enjoyed singing together—occasionally while at parties, but mostly when out with friends. On weekends when my father wasn't on the boat, they would often relax at a place on Mastic Road called John's Riviera Restaurant and Bar, just a couple of miles from our home. John's might have been like the bar on the TV show *Cheers*, where, as the theme song says, "everybody knows your name." The regulars knew my parents. They knew their names and enjoyed hearing them sing duets. Someone would always end up requesting, "C'mon, Al and Anne, sing for us."

When it came to parenting, my father was cold and detached, much like his own father. I was 10 and in the fifth grade when he died. In all of that time, he had spoken directly to me only a few times. One night, he sat at dinner, talking to my mother from his end of the table to hers. He paused long enough for me to think that he had finished speaking, so I started to talk, only to be startled when he cut me off with a gruff, "Be quiet. I'm talking."

Both male and female robins guard the nest from danger. In about 10 days the babies are fully feathered. Their wings develop so fast that it takes only two weeks for them to learn to fly alone.

Our family was changing. By 1958 my oldest brother, Al, was married, had an infant daughter, and worked with my father on the tugboat. John was in the army. Anne, Bob, and Bill attended high school. I was in fifth grade; Liz, third; Patty, kindergarten. My mother was pregnant with her ninth child.

Ten days before Michael was born, tragedy struck our family. My father and brother Al died when their tugboat sank during a storm. It happened in the Long Island Sound, near the Stepping Stone Lighthouse offshore of Great Neck. My father was 41; my brother, 21.

When it came time to bury my father, my mother faced the additional challenge of persuading the Catholic cemetery to bury him alongside my brother. She argued that he had fathered nine children who had all been raised Catholic.

It is hard for me to understand such callousness. My father had stood off the altar with my mother when they had married. Their family-planning was limited, as they used just the one method of church-approved birth control. And, throughout the years, my father ate as we did: a lot of meatless-Friday meals. I might have missed it, but I've never once heard that my father spoke against the religion that my mother so faithfully observed.

Robins are monogamous during the entire breeding season, but a female may look for a new mate if something happens to her first mate.

My parents had been married for only 22 years. My mother lived to be 88 and never remarried.

Months after my father died, I sat alone in the living room, playing with the cat. My mother had been at the kitchen table, reading the newspaper, when she came and asked, "What bus do you take?"

I told her.

"Did the bus driver ever touch you?"

I told her.

"Why didn't you ever tell me? Your father would have killed him."

Not telling is never right. But, if there's a silver lining, and my mother was right: Perhaps my silence saved my father from murdering a man.

Robins make different sounds to communicate. When a predator is near, they emit a warning call. When a nest or an individual robin feels threatened, it makes a sound similar to a horse whinnying. During the nesting season, robins make a high-pitched sound, especially when they see a hawk or other birds of prey. In response to this call, other robins will repeat the sound and stay still.

My father and the bus driver had actually come face to face once, but I had been silent. Normally, the bus dropped me off on the main road and I'd walk about a half mile to our house. This day, I happened to be the last one on the bus. I was a shy girl who showed adults respect and obeyed unquestioningly, so when the abusive bus driver said, "Show me where you live," I directed him off the regular route to my home.

He stopped the bus in front of my house. I don't know what he planned to do with the knowledge of where I lived, but, I don't think that he anticipated what he found when we got to the house.

My father was working on his car on the side of our quiet road. He looked out from under the hood and waved to the driver.

"It looked like rain," the bus driver said, "so I thought I'd bring her to the house."

"Thanks," my father replied.

I walked past my father to the house without exchanging a greeting.

I never learned the details of what my mother read in the paper that day. I only learned by surmising from that brief exchange that I hadn't been the only victim. I wondered, "Who else—and who told?"

I believe because of where my father was that day—a visible presence facing a sinister bus driver—that he unwittingly saved me from further abuse. Where was Dad that day? Right where I needed him.

I went through a time when I blocked my father out of my life so intensely that I couldn't even picture his face. It was not the relationship that I wanted with him, even in his death. I think my relationship with him began changing when I sat in church one day and saw Mary, an older woman, sitting several pews ahead of me. Her frail, elderly father, Carl, sat next to her. I watched as Mary gently fussed with Carl's jacket, resting it comfortably over his shoulders. I imagined my father old and frail like Carl, and I imagined myself trying to make him comfortable. I saw him changed. He was old, gentle, and approachable.

Later, at home, I stood on the back deck and cried quietly. It was good. I could see my father's face again. I had made peace with him and could finally tell him that I love him.

Does it matter now?

It does to me. For me, relationships don't end when loved ones are on The Other Side. We can send love—and receive it.

Birds of a feather flock together. It's true of robins—and of most of us, I believe.

Jack was one of my father's closest friends, one whom I knew personally. They had worked together on the tugs. He was godfather to two of my siblings. Outwardly, at least, he and my father seemed quite different. Jack was soft spoken and warm, an attentive family man. When he and his wife, Kay, visited, they brought their children with them. They had two boys. That was it. They were a calm presence in our chaotic family life. I suspect Jack was the kind of man who would use good judgment when it came to choosing a friend, and I trust that he found honorable qualities in my father.

My mother gave my father's diary to my brother Michael, the youngest brother who never knew our father. Michael wrote this to me about the father he had never met—the father I lived with, but didn't know: "He is owed an honest assessment—or maybe we owe it to ourselves—with a dose of forgiveness standing by for the faults that we discover. He gave me a love of history and the culture of his times, because that's how I first set about trying to know him."

My father knew about waterways, navigation, and other maritime activities that intrigue me. And he sang. It's a little thing, but I like it. I don't have the voice either one of my parents had, but I enjoy singing. I take comfort in this quote by Henry Van Dyke: "The woods would be quiet if no bird sang but the one that sang best."

One of my favorite songs from my parents' generation is "The Glory of Love," sung by the late Jimmy Durante:

> You've got to give a little, take a little and let your poor heart break a little.
> That's the story of, that's the glory of love.
> You've got to laugh a little, cry a little, until the clouds roll by a little.
> That's the story of, that's the glory of love.

It's the first week of June, and I'm watching the baby robins from my bedroom window as they stretch their mouths open wide to be fed. I tell my granddaughter, Madison, to climb on a chair and observe quietly. With my words and actions, I attempt to convey that we're privileged to witness such tender care. I take none of it for granted. Not the closeness to nature, the secure nest, or the tenderness.

But nature isn't always as gentle as a mama robin in a nest. Sometimes its harshness can be disturbing, as unsettling as a father who never gets to know a child's love for him, a father who was fitted with emotional armor as a child that he never gave up, one who didn't notice the armor wasn't at all useful, a father whose time was too short for some of life's lessons.

Last week I asked my father's 92-year-old sister, Grace, what word or words come to mind when she thinks of her brother, my father.

"Friendly and fun," she said.

"Really?" I responded, sounding a little like Amy Poehler on *Saturday Night Live.*

The first time I saw the bird sitting in the nest, I wondered what kind of bird it was. As if on cue, she ruffled her feathers in such a way as to show me the rust color on her belly.

With my father, it wasn't as simple. I never got to see what was beneath the rough surface. In spite of his flaws—flaws that saddened and distressed me and others, I believe that he was a good, loving man.

Really.

June 2012

"I grew up with six brothers.
That's how I learned to dance—waiting for the bathroom."
—Bob Hope

Dance

The October air should have been crisp, but we were having a warmer than usual fall here on the North Fork of Long Island. Tom and I had errands to do on Love Lane in Mattituck. If we have to be out for errands in any weather, Love Lane is one of our favorite places. Our granddaughter, Madison, two-and-a-half, was with us. All things considered, we weren't in a hurry to get home.

As we left Orlowski's Hardware Store, I looked across the street at the dance studio. "Let's take a walk over," I suggested.

Inside, we heard classical music, the kind that makes my shoulders drop and my face muscles relax. With permission from the woman behind the desk, the three of us—Tom, Madison, and I—watched through double glass doors. A dancer of about nine years old was in the midst of a private lesson. When Tom and I were ready to leave, Madison still appeared mesmerized by the young ballerina. We stayed, watched some more, and then inquired, "Are there classes for children as young as Madison?"

There were: Madison could join a class on Saturday mornings, from 9:15 to 10. But with only one student in the class—a girl who would soon turn three—the class probably would be cancelled soon.

Interrupting her focus on the dancer, I asked Madison, "Would you like to come here and dance, too?"

Madison didn't hesitate to tell us that she would. We checked with her parents, Zac and Michelle, and, with their OK, we registered Madison for lessons. We bought her a colorful leotard and pink ballet slippers, and, when we arrived with Madison that first Saturday morning, we learned that the other little girl was sick. That meant it was just the dance teacher Gretchen and Madison.

But they weren't alone on the dance floor. Madison felt she needed us—me and Tom—not just in the room, but right next to her doing whatever steps she did.

I'm pretty sure Tom's time with Madison at ballet class, tap-tap-tapping his pointed toe, has been his only experience with ballet. We keep finding out how flexible grandparents can be, in more ways than one.

I never took dance classes as a child, but when I was in my 30s, I saw an ad for a ballet class for adult beginners. One night a week, for six weeks, a group of five women who had never met before, made a serious attempt to do a little ballet dancing. I remember lining up at one end of the dance floor, each of us waiting our turn to leap and hop to the other side. With one arm stretched out in front, one stretched behind, we attempted a sequence of graceful leaps punctuated with a hop and a charming turn of the head. We moved across the vast dance floor, solo, with a hope and a prayer that we weren't in the middle of a leap when we reached the wall.

One of my favorite children's books, *Song and Dance Man* by Karen Ackerman, begins, "Grandpa was a song and dance man who once danced on the vaudeville stage. When we visit, he tells us about a time before people watched TV, back in the good old days, the song and dance days." In the story, Grandpa and his three grandchildren go to the attic, where he finds his old tap shoes, bowler hat, and a cane. They clear some space, and then, "it's show time."

Years ago, when I was in my 50s, I learned about a tap-dancing class for women. It was already a full class of 30 or more, so I felt lucky to join. We met in the quaint Poquatuck Hall in Orient. It wasn't easy learning the steps, but it was a fun experience.

Like Madison loving her very own ballet slippers, I love the fact that I have my very own shiny black tap shoes. I put them on a few months ago, under the pretense of entertaining Madison. We had a grand time. I didn't have a bowler hat or a cane, as the grandfather in *Song and Dance Man* had, and I sure didn't have his dance skills. And although my audience was just a third of his, she was no less enthusiastic.

I care for Madison two days a week and remember when she moved from long stretches of sleep to more awake time. I did what is recommended: I fed her, changed her, and read her a story. One day she looked up at me from her little bouncy seat as if to say, "So? Now what?" And that's when the dancing began.

"Well," I responded, "I'll put on some music and see where that goes." I felt like dancing, so I did.

Someone says we should dance as though no one is watching. I danced like no one, Madison included, was watching. My audience of one was thrilled and wanted more. I obliged. And that became our routine on Monday and Friday mornings.

But things changed quickly. Soon I didn't have an audience; I had a dance partner. We've had our favorite CDs, among them, *Fleetwood Mac's Greatest Hits* and the soundtrack from *Mamma Mia!* More recently, we've added Ziggy Marley's *Family Time* to the favorites. I put a basket on a shelf within Madison's reach, and, now and then, I add something to enhance dance time—maracas, tambourines, a xylophone, a triangle, and a drum.

It's been fun and heartwarming to see that, even when she had a vocabulary of about a half dozen words, Madison could get even the stodgiest adult up and dancing. She did it on Sundays when the extended family came for dinner. She did it at Thanksgiving with people she'd never met before. She did it with anyone, anytime we had music playing.

We still dance, Madison and I, although now her interests have broadened. And dancing is just one of many things she enjoys doing and involving others in doing with her. Sometimes, on a morning when she arrives, I'm tired. And, sometimes, she's not quite ready to release her parents to their workday. I hit the play button for a CD, and a quote by Austrian writer Vicki Baum comes to life for us: "There are shortcuts to happiness, and dancing is one of them."

Our daughter Kim took classes in jazz dancing. She was much older than Madison is now. One year, the June dance recital fell on Kim's 14th birthday. She loved her birthdays and looked forward to them with great anticipation.

On the day before the recital, we needed to go to Riverhead for dress rehearsal and pictures. I was in the car waiting for Kim. Not wanting to be late, I was relieved when I finally saw her come through the front door. I realized that I hadn't seen her dance costume on her until then.

"Oh. Wow," I said to myself when I saw her. She had pulled her strawberry blond hair back in a bun. A headpiece was tilted to one side with its black feathers resting against her face. She wore black fishnet stockings and chunky, black, low-heeled jazz shoes. The costume's sleeves were long, puffy, and sheer black. A yellow leotard added color and fit snugly against her slender torso.

"Just once," I thought, as I watched Kim walk to the car, "I'd love to dress like that." As Kim got closer, I saw something else that she was wearing: a look of misery. Perplexed, I asked gently, "Honey, what's wrong? You look so unhappy."

She shot a brisk answer back at me. "You wanna know what's wrong? I'll tell you what's wrong. I'm gonna be 14 tomorrow. I have braces, glasses, and I'm dressed like a banana."

My instincts told me quickly, "Don't laugh." I focused on driving, while the top half of my body shook, wanting so badly to release a big guffaw. We drove the seven miles from our home in Laurel to Riverhead in silence. Pictures from the day show that somehow Kim cured the mood, dropped the miserable look, and smiled big.

When I was in college at Long Island University in Southampton, I organized a dance night out with a group of girlfriends. We planned a night at a club in Westhampton. It was my college roommate and close friend Sue's birthday. Five of us stood around the dance floor enjoying the music and waiting for guys to ask us to dance. Imagine: No matter how strongly we felt the rhythm of the music and how much we wanted to move to it, we didn't. We waited. Withholding the joyful expression of dance, there we stood, waiting for someone of the opposite sex to approach us and ask if we wanted to dance.

Of course, we wanted to dance. We were bursting to dance. How sad and appalling that we waited. Good riddance to those times.

The first girl in the group who was asked to dance turned to the one closest to her and asked, "Could you hold my pocketbook?" The second girl who was asked to dance made the same request of the one of us standing closest. Same with the third. When the fourth girl was asked, she handed her own bag, as well as the others that she was holding, to the last in the group: Sue.

Sue always got a lot of attention on our small campus. She was a terrific cheerleader, a great dancer, cute, petite, smart, and fun. Maybe the dim lights in the club, and where she stood in the group, caused her to go unnoticed. The rest of us were having our chance to dance, but Sue, weighed down with handbags, looked less and less approachable.

The birthday girl stood on the edge of the dance floor, looking forlorn and abandoned. With all of our purses dangling from both her arms, she might as well have been imitating a coat rack. Forty-five years later, she hasn't let me forget that birthday.

At some point during my elementary school years, our physical education class included dance lessons. I recall learning square dancing and the polka. My square dance skills have rusted over the years from lack of use. But I married into a Polish family, so I've had opportunities to brush up on my polka.

Celebrations feel more complete if we've danced to at least one good jumpy polka that leaves us breathless and wanting more. At our son Jeremy's wedding, when the band played a polka, Tom and I spun our way around the dance floor. When Tom changes our dance direction, it usually means that we're in for a spin. I hold tight and sometimes even let out a little high-pitched "Woo!" like his parents used to.

I was surprised when Jess and Jeremy showed us their wedding pictures. The photographer had captured us on the move, my left foot kicking out from under my long, full-skirted dress. Tom and I are looking into each other's eyes. We're smiling. We look as though we're in an ad, promoting, "Be Happy. Do the Polka."

If I saw such a picture of another couple, I'd enjoy it, for the tender look they seemed to exchange. There was more behind that look for us: There weren't many people on the dance floor, and we were moving quite fast. I'm sure I stayed locked in eye contact with Tom for purely practical reasons. I was looking for assurance that he was getting my firm message: "You loosen your grip, buddy, and you're in big trouble."

Jeremy and I had one of those special dances for just the groom and his mom. He chose one of my favorite songs, "What a Wonderful World." I was hoping that we'd have a chance to practice for even five minutes before the wedding day, but that didn't happen.

When I've watched mothers and sons dance as we would, I often wondered what they say to each other. They always look like they're dancing and chatting comfortably. I've imagined different conversations, such as, "Thank you for the chance to have this closeness with you, dancing to a song that you chose for us." Or maybe, "The food was good, wasn't it? Even Uncle Jake said so, and you know how he can be."

I don't know, of course, what others have talked about while sharing that sentimental time. Jeremy and I wondered together if our feet were in sync. I recall him asking, "Did we start off right?" I wasn't sure that we had. At times, it felt as though we had some missteps. But neither of us suggested stopping and starting over. I, at least, had the benefit of my long dress covering my feet. Our dance ended, and we hugged warmly—no practice needed.

Through the years, Tom and I have taken ballroom dance classes a couple of times. I knew the lindy from my early teens. I saw my older siblings do it, and I learned from a friend. We all watched the popular TV show, *Band Stand*, after school. When the participants did fast dancing, they did the lindy.

When I danced with my younger sister, Liz, I always led, so that was part of what Tom and I had to work on in our lessons: letting him lead. Whenever we're out together where there's dance music, I'm eager to get up and dance. Sometimes I feel the need to remind Tom, "C'mon, we have to dance—while all our parts are still working."

If it's a slow dance, before getting on the floor, we're often in discussion. "What is this?" Tom might ask, meaning, is it a foxtrot? A waltz? Something else? We didn't take enough lessons—or practice enough—for it to matter. We generally do the same steps for every slow song, anyway.

I don't like it when I hear someone say, "I can't dance." I'm convinced dancing is part of our nature. It seems to me, it's a matter of choice. Either we stay open to that part of us, or we shut it down. I think about a plaque that I have on the wall. It's a Native American design on a flat stone piece that says, "Your feet can learn the steps, but only your spirit can dance." I think dancing is good for us mentally, physically, and spiritually.

Often when people pass on, the family gathers after the funeral to share a meal. After my mother-in-law's funeral and the luncheon that followed, a couple of her grandchildren drove to a tattoo parlor and had an angel and the Polish word for "family" forever imprinted on their backs. I'd like my grandchildren to know that I'd love for them to gather in my memory, but to skip the tattoo. My thinking could change with time, but I have high regard for skin as an important organ and I can't reconcile using it for art. I say, that's what frames and walls are for. And, knowing my mother-in-law, I think she would have agreed. I like the song, "I Hope You Dance" with the lyrics, "When you get the choice to sit it out or dance, I hope you dance." The song's meaning goes beyond putting feet to dance floor. For my intentions, I find the simple words in the title sufficient. I'd be honored if, after my passing, my family and friends chose a place where they could gather to eat—and dance. Try my tap shoes. Lead or follow in a lindy. Tap your foot or sway, if that's all you can do. Alone or with a crowd, I hope they know the joy of dancing as if no one is watching. I should tell them now: I happen to like my dance music loud. So, if you find something odd going on with the volume, that might be me. I hope that no one will mind. I'll be dancing along, unseen, from The Other Side.

2011

"So, let us not be blind to our differences—but let us also direct attention to our common interests and to the means by which those differences can be resolved."
—President John F. Kennedy,
Commencement Speech at American University,
June 10, 1963

Campaign 2008

Earlier this month, my husband and I knocked on the doors of undecided voters in Pennsylvania. It seemed at first that volunteering meant giving something up—our comfort zone, as well as the time and expense of traveling five hours each way. But the people who spoke to us put a face on the issues in this election.

There was the guy in his 50s who told us this is the first time he's been out of a job since he was 16 years old. Very soon, his unemployment benefits will run out. He figures some kind of welfare is next.

The woman younger than us and toothless didn't talk about health insurance. She's worried about her son who, she said, will likely go to a war that the United States started in the wrong way and in the wrong country.

Raymond said he's going to make a statement and vote for Nader. He showed us the solar collectors on his house, something Tom and I have in common with him. We talked about energy policies and asked him to vote, this time to make a difference.

Jennifer was disgusted after a long, difficult struggle to get health insurance for her four-year-old daughter.

A young black man with a South African accent was the only person to mention Obama's race. He won't vote for a black man, he said, just because he's black. We talked about the poverty in our wealthy country, agreeing on the need for early childhood education and nutritious meals for poor children.

He brought up the subject of abortion, saying he favored McCain's idea of giving the issue back to the states. We talked about a family whose daughter was pregnant at 13, devastating her and her parents – all observant Catholics. They agonized and they grieved, and acted on their decision as quickly as they could. Had the procedure been illegal in their state, they would have traveled to another state, or to another country. Because this young man and I were respectful of one another, we were able to have a calm discussion.

Another young man stood out. When we asked if he was registered to vote, he replied, "I'm a Republican. My dad's a Republican, so that's what I am."

When asked about an issue that was important to him, he could only shrug.

"What about the war?"

"It's not a real war," he said.

Gripping my clipboard tighter, I told him it's dreadfully real. I mentioned the men and women who are serving, who have been injured, who have died.

"They shouldn't have signed up for the military," he said.

Nothing moved him. He believed his life was unaffected by any issue mentioned. Sadly, he represents far too many eligible voters in our country – crossing all ages and party affiliations. We moved on.

As is often the case with volunteering, we didn't give up anything compared to what the people we met gave us – a deeper commitment to make a difference in this election and pride in the democratic process.

2008

> *"Christmas never would have caught on if it had been called 'Celebrate a Little Jew's Birthday.'"*
> —Andrew Borowitz

Christmas: A Little This, A Little That

A few nights ago, I washed dishes the old-fashioned way: using the sink, water from the faucet, green dish soap, a dish cloth, and my hands. I thought of that old commercial that ran quite often when I was kid. It showed two hands and asked viewers to identify which belonged to the mom and which to her adult daughter. I always looked for a clue to the right answer.

Thanks to the kind of dish soap the mom used for washing the family's dishes—that is, all of the dishes that the whole family dirtied, but only she washed—we could not tell her hands from her daughter's.

The next time I see my daughter, we'll put our hands together, her 28-year-old hands and mine with its knobby fingers. I can't wait to see who we fool.

I was washing the dishes by hand because our dishwasher had stopped working. I don't mind washing dishes sometimes. Water often stimulates my thinking. But on this night I had turned on the kitchen TV. It was the night of the lighting of the Christmas tree in Rockefeller Center. I would be doing a mundane task, but I'd also hear joyful sounds of holiday songs and music. I imagined families across the nation tuning in. I remember being flexible with our kids' bedtimes so they could watch some of the holiday TV specials.

The show opened with a song by a young, contemporary singer. She appeared on the outdoor stage in a man-made winter scene, surrounded by glitz and all things artificial. I don't recall anything about the song that she sang, whether it was a cute catchy tune, or an inspirational message. It seemed to be all about a provocative look in a make-believe scene.

When I looked up from the bubbles in the dishwater to the TV, I saw more bubbles: big, round bubbles that formed cleavage. Now, it could be that I missed the good parts of this holiday special—although I did catch a snippet of the legendary Tony Bennett—but what I saw were pretentious performances that seemed to strive to imitate gaiety.

I thought about the value of PBS. But I wasn't tuned in to channel 13 or channel 21. The exuberant, young crowd that had gathered for this tree-lighting special seemed pleased. Maybe they saw the same gaudy glitz that I saw. And maybe, from their perspective, the lighting was simply a seasonal event, something exciting and uplifting.

I found myself groaning and asking myself, "This is Christmas? What the heck is Christmas, anyway?"

Oh, I know what it is *supposed* to be. Growing up Catholic when I did, I hadn't been familiar with much of the Bible. But the story of Jesus's birth was one that we heard in church every December. The church would be packed—every seat taken—many people standing in the aisles. For some, Christmas was one of two days when they went to church, and then, it was all about gifts, cookies, and stress. Lots of stress.

When asked, I guess a lot of people would say that Christmas is a religious holiday. But more prominently, it is a celebration of Santa Claus and great sales. Sometimes I even wonder why the tree-lighting event includes songs about Bethlehem and peace. It becomes a hodgepodge of a message.

Our daughter, Kim, once shared a comic strip with me whose caption read, "Who Really Killed Jesus?" The panel showed a police lineup with four suspects: Jews, Romans, Karl Marx, and Santa Claus. The guilty one, of course, was dear old Santa.

If I had been asked as a child whom I trusted more—Jesus or Santa Claus—it would have been Jesus. All of the Christmas hype encouraged us to believe in a Santa who paid attention to letters and wishes of good little boys and girls. That didn't work in my life. No matter how good I was—and I was pretty darn good—the magic didn't happen.

What I had heard about Jesus resonated with me. Unlike the North Pole crew, Jesus didn't have a lot of stuff. I liked hearing that he lived a simple life, that he worked relentlessly to help the poor and others who were marginalized. He lived a life of deep compassion, and he spoke and taught about peace. When I included Jesus in my prayers or meditations, I had a peaceful experience.

But sometime in my 20s, things changed. In many ways, I had become less hopeful and more discouraged about life in general.

Simultaneously, the born-again movement entered our culture. For some, it was a time of spiritual renewal. For me, its messages were fear-based, heavy on judgment, and exclusion. I had no connection at all with the Jesus that was talked about. I even disliked hearing his name. I guess I made him guilty by association.

Reverend Dr. Martin Luther King Jr.—one of our country's greatest— emulated the Jesus that I knew. King was a compassionate, incredibly courageous man. He envisioned change that would make all of us better people, and America a better country.

I'm sure his wife, Coretta Scott King, was pleased when the federal government designated King's birthday, January 15, a national holiday. Many church services honor King's memory on, at least, one day in January. And, every January, I'm awestruck when, at our North Fork Unitarian-Universalist Fellowship, Jere Jacob recites King's *I Have a Dream* speech.

King's lifework is talked about on TV news shows and special programs, on the radio, and in schools. National Public Radio airs poetry recitations. Children read books about him. It is all so fitting for a man who taught the inspiring lessons of justice, nonviolence, peace, and love.

It is debatable whether or not Jesus had a wife, but we know that he had a mother. So let's have a talk with his mother, Mary. Not the blonde-haired, blue-eyed Mary whose blue robe matches her eyes. The real Mary. The dark-haired one with the olive complexion. The Jewish Mom.

It's today. Somehow, mysteriously, Mary and I meet. She says to me, "Mary Ellen—by the way, I like your name—look, Jewish mothers, I know they get a bad rap, but, honey, we need to talk. I know a lot of Jewish mothers think that their sons are to die for. But hear me out. Here, in eternity, I see a lot of people. I am green with envy for Martin Luther King Jr.'s mother—and for other mothers, too. Chris Columbus's. George Washington's. Abe Lincoln's.

"Just once, if my kid—my Jesus—could get the kind of treatment those guys get: The post office closes, schools shut down—and people know why. They tune into NPR and hear poetry only about their boys, about Martin and Chris and George and Abe.

"Everyone, every year, remembers all of the great things that Martin did in his 39 years of life. My boy, Jesus, he doesn't get even one day.

Not one. After all he did so that people would notice the poor, after all he did so that people would talk about peace, love, justice. My boy. He was so brave and so good."

And I say, "Maaary, excuse me, have you heard of Christmas? The world-wide celebration of your kid's birth? We listen to stories about his birth. We sing about it. We decorate for it. We go all out."

"But you don't feel it," she interrupts. "You don't say what you say about Martin. You don't say, 'Wow. What a brave, gutsy guy. He tried so hard to fight against injustices, to help the poor, to speak on behalf of peace.' You hear about his life and you think, 'Yeah, yeah, yeah. Blah, blah, blah.'

"Mary Ellen—I really like your name—it is no surprise that Christmas isn't about my boy. It's about a fat white guy who brings rich kids big gifts and poor kids few or no gifts. What an insult to my boy to mix his celebration with that.

"Just one day. That's all. Something like what Martin has. The schools close. The post office closes, maybe just for half a day, even. Maya Angelou could read some poetry on the radio. There could be a moment of silence at the United Nations. You know, something where people really stop and take a minute to think about my boy's lifework. Just one day, you know, Mare? Is that too much for a mother to ask?"

My childhood was emotionally turbulent. My feeling connected to the spirit of Jesus was a light in dark times.

When Tom and I married, we hadn't yet found Unitarian-Universalism. Neither of us was interested in attending any kind of church, but I still felt connected to Jesus. The social activist Jesus. The one that folk singer and anti-war activist, Joan Baez and others sang about.

In the church on our wedding day, Tom and I walked each other down the aisle. The song that I chose—and that Tom went along with—was Joan Baez's rendition of "Just a Closer Walk with Thee." My nieces and nephews—there were about a dozen of them, ranging in ages from 5 to 15—took part in our ceremony. They sat to the side like a choir. Tom sang and played the guitar, and they sang with him.

The lyrics of one song—"They'll Know We Are Christians By Our Love"—say, "We'll guard each one's dignity and save each one's pride." Of course, that's a farce in many churches that call themselves Christian. It was the case during the Civil Rights Movement, when churches were segregated, and it still is today, for other reasons. I'm certain that Jesus wouldn't want anything to do with some so-called Christian churches, past and present.

As for the tree-lighting ceremony with the make-believe everything, I'm wondering if Jesus might have began a campaign to *plant* a tree at Rockefeller Center, a tree that grew with the special honor of being exquisitely decorated from one year to the next.

Instead, every year, we learn about the chosen tree: That it lived for decades, reached a great height, survived storms, and provided lasting memories. And then, the tree earns the ultimate reward: Chop, chop. You're dead.

I love the traditional Christmas Eve dinner that Tom and I share with part of his family. It is simple and authentic. Generally, things go rather predictably with few surprises. This year, it is our turn to host. The other two families—Tom's sister's and his cousin's—will arrive promptly at the designated time. They'll bring dishes of food, some to be warmed, some ready for the table.

We'll break a wafer called an oplatek, and each of us will receive a small piece. The oplatek will be small, but big enough to share. We will all greet each person with "Merry Christmas" or "God Bless You" or, if the holidays overlap, "Happy Hanukkah." As we greet, we break off a small, sometimes minuscule, piece of each other's oplatek. It's all about the symbolism of seeing each person present, giving, and receiving.

To some of us, the Polish meal is a once-a-year treat of delicious, traditional food. Others who are less interested in the different tastes find something to pick at, but no one ever leaves the table hungry. I'll always remember the first time that I attended this tradition. The night had many firsts for me, including the first time I had ever seen so many homemade cookies on one table.

After dessert we move into the living room. Someone hands out old faded sheet music. We will sing 20 or so carols. Cousin Don will play his accordion; Tom, his guitar. We will give Michael, a cousin who is developmentally delayed, our undivided attention when he sings "Jingle Bells" solo. Tom will sing "Silent Night," something that his mother, especially, enjoyed. It's a highlight of the night for me, too.

Maybe our kids will take their kids to the Christmas tree-lighting in New York City. Maybe they will be among the cheering crowds on a cold night as the majestic evergreen is lit and admired.

I love seeing the tree. What is disconcerting to me is the fanfare of a TV special that lacks authenticity.

For their holiday celebrations, my kids will all find what's meaningful for them and their families. I do hope they will find time for the simple joys—food, music, storytelling—something that merits repeating one year to the next, one generation to the next.

I find what some have done to the teachings of Jesus appalling. I'm able to honor him because I keep him totally separate from their made-up stuff. Franciscan, Richard Rohr, describes "what Jesus spent most of his time doing: touching and healing people, doing acts of justice and inclusion, teaching and living ways of compassion and non-violence." That's who I celebrate.

Christmas is different things to different people. Sometimes it's a blend of things: a little Jesus here, a little Santa there. For some, it's all sales, all Santa.

Nothing wrong with that. I guess it's a matter of what feels genuine. Gift-giving is a lovely thing, especially when it comes from the heart. But I also think it's too bad Jesus can't get a day all his own, when we hear about his life and his work in poetry and song, a day that a Jewish mother—or any mother—would feel good about.

2008

Update: Before Tom's mother passed on, she sang the Polish carols. Tom's father, Aunt Bonnie and Uncle Lew are left nostalgic for that tradition. We try humming them. The best we can do is belt out a strong refrain: GLORIA! The faded Christmas song sheets have a fresher look now. Winter and Hanukkah songs have been added, as well as two more guitarists: our son Jeremy and brother-in-law Rich.

At the Unitarian-Universalist church in Southold. The religious education classes shared their family's Christmas traditions with the congregation. Jeremy, Kim and Zac made their presentations in traditional Polish attire.

*"Few are those who see with their own eyes
and feel with their own hearts."*

—*Albert Einstein*

Gutsy Little Gracie

I belong to a church that's part of the denomination with the cumbersome name of Unitarian-Universalism (UU). We hold services in a charming building, a church built in 1731 as a meeting house for Puritans, Congregationalists, and other church groups. There are many outstanding ministers in the UU denomination, ministers who have been trained in the finest seminaries in this country, including Union Theological Seminary in New York City, Meadville Lombard Theological School in Chicago, and the seminaries at Harvard and Yale.

Our little church group is too small to support a minister. But every Sunday, there's a speaker in our pulpit; lately it's people from our own congregation. They either write something themselves or they read a sermon written by a UU minister and provided by the Church of the Larger Fellowship (CLF). The CLF's mission is to provide a ministry to isolated religious liberals. You can be isolated alone in your home or isolated in a group, as we are in Jamesport, Long Island.

Over the years, we've had some regulars in our pulpit—a Buddhist, a retired Presbyterian minister, and a couple of UU intern ministers, including my daughter. They have all inspired me.

A few months ago, I shared a sermon written by my friend Maureen's minister, Deborah Lindsay, a United Church of Christ minister in Ohio. Her sermon spoke in favor of an Islamic cultural center planned for Lower Manhattan. Now it's called "Park51" for its address at 51 Park Place. The plan is for it to be 13 stories high. The majority of the center will be open to the general public—its proponents saying it'll promote interfaith dialogue. The multi-faith part of the design includes a 500-seat auditorium, a theater, a performing arts center, a fitness center, a swimming pool, a basketball court, a child-care area, a bookstore, a culinary school, an art studio, a food court, and a memorial to the victims of the September 11 attacks. Prayer space for the Muslim community will accommodate 1,000 to 2,000 people.

Several weeks after I shared Reverend Lindsay's sermon, a mom in our congregation approached me and said, "We have to tell you what happened this week in Gracie's classroom." Gracie, a sixth grader, had a substitute teacher. The subject of Park51 came up, and the substitute expressed her disapproval of it. She asked the sixth graders how they felt about the issue: "Raise your hand," she said, "if you disapprove of this project, too." Hands went up. Many hands. Then she said, "Raise your hand if you think it should be built." One student raised her hand: Gracie.

The substitute teacher looked at Gracie and said with a strong tone of disbelief, "You're in favor of it?"

Being alone with her hand raised was bad enough. Now, Gracie had to actually use her voice to respond to an incredulous adult and to her classmates, who had chimed in to echo the substitute's question with their own versions of "You're in favor of it?"

I've told Gracie that I'm proud of her, and I know others did, too. Perhaps our little congregation and our Unitarian-Universalist denomination can take a bit of the credit. This might be what Unitarian minister William Ellery Channing was talking about in the early 1800s when he wrote "The Great End in Religious Instruction."

Channing wrote,

> *The great end in religious instruction is not to stamp our minds upon the young, but to stir up their own; Not to make them see with our eyes, but to look inquiringly and steadily with their own; Not to give them a definite amount of knowledge, but to inspire a fervent love of truth;*
> *Not to form an outward regularity, but to touch inward springs;*
> *Not to bind them by ineradicable prejudices to our particular sect or peculiar notions, but to prepare them for impartial, conscientious judging of whatever subjects may be offered to their decision;*
> *Not to burden the memory, but to quicken and strengthen the power of thought;*
> *Not to impose religion upon them in the form of arbitrary rules, but to awaken the conscience, the moral discernment.*

In a word, the great end is to awaken the soul, to excite and cherish spiritual life.

Channing came from a prominent family in Boston with a grandfather who signed the Declaration of Independence. He was known as a champion of human rights, promoting social reform in areas of free speech, education, peace, relief for the poor, and anti-slavery. Ralph Waldo Emerson called Channing "a kind of public Conscience."

I love the beach, so I enjoyed learning that Channing once spoke to his congregation about the influence a particular beach had on him: "No spot on earth has helped to form me so much as that beach. . . . There, in reverential sympathy with the mighty power around me, I became conscious of power within."

I think it's a good idea to check in with my fairness meter every once in a while, so I asked myself, "What if all the other children had expressed their *approval* of the Islamic center and Gracie had been alone in expressing disapproval of it? Would I still want to celebrate her lack of intimidation? Would I be just as glad for her strength of spirit? How would I have felt and responded to Gracie's individualism if her steadfast views did not match mine?"

I hope I would have engaged Gracie in conversation about how she formed her opinion. Then, I hope I would have said, "Well, we feel differently about this, but it sounds as though you've thought it through, and that's something to feel good about." That is my hope because we need our young people to be thinkers, as Channing said, "to look inquiringly and steadily with their own eyes."

I didn't form my own opinion immediately about the proposed Islamic center. When it comes to forming opinions or making decisions, I don't know if I struggle more than others do. If I appear fickle or indecisive, it might be the influence of my zodiac sign, Libra. The scales, Libra's symbol, represent balance, harmony and a sense of fair play. Keeping those scales in balance can be challenging. For some issues, I draw on my gut reaction and try to listen to my heart, as well.

Those tools work best when it's a personal matter. But something like Park51 has a broad impact. It involves an array of sensitive issues. I read various sources, listened carefully, and formed my opinion. I wondered how the sixth graders in Gracie's class formed their opinions. From the news that's on the televisions and radios in their homes? From family discussions? From their churches? When I read the sermon written by Reverend Lindsay, Gracie was in her religious education class, but her mom had been present.

I remember while in my early teens hearing Reverend Dr. Martin Luther King Jr. on the TV in our home. An older brother made a disparaging comment about King's efforts to change America. My mother and I were the only other ones home. I don't know how my mother felt, since she didn't say anything one way or the other. I didn't say anything either, but my gut and my heart told me that my brother's assessment was wrong and unjust, although I didn't use words like "unjust" at the time.

Many had opinions that changed with time. I don't know what caused my brother and me to, initially, form different opinions about civil rights in America. We'd been raised in the same home, gone to the same school, and had been taken to the same church. We were a Catholic family, and no one was given a choice: On Sunday mornings, we went to church. I liked some of the ritual, and I also liked the Jesus I imagined. His message of love, peace, and justice resonated with me.

I left Catholicism as a young adult, but I kept my image of Jesus. I even remember thinking of him when I heard the song from the 1960s, "He Ain't Heavy, He's My Brother." And then, along came the far-right Christian groups that ruined our relationship. They found him, remade him, and I let him go. I had to. They had him all mixed in with their negativism and homophobia. It took a while for me to work things out and fit him in with my expanding spirituality. The separation didn't do either one of us any harm. We're both still just fine.

I have a page from a magazine ad on my file cabinet. I don't know what it was advertising. I cut that part off. The part I saved is a picture of a forest with three words in the middle of the picture: "Never be intimidated." Gracie is a sweet, respectful girl. There's nothing at all brazen or harsh about her. Yet, I'm more than 50 years older than she is, and I'm still working on speaking my mind in a calm way without being defensive or offensive and without feeling intimidated. I'm reminded of one of the few full sentences I know in Spanish: "Es mejor tarde que nunca." Better late than never.

2010

"My religion is very simple. My religion is kindness."
—Dali Lama

Worth and Dignity, Homemade

I thought of my mother-in-law, Louise, recently, when I did something that she would have never done: I took a pie crust from the freezer. Her pie crusts—like her jams, pickles, and other specialties—were always homemade.

Without realizing it, my mother-in-law intimidated me in many ways. She was just being who she was. In my early days of parenting, Louise gave me a decorative plate that read, "A good mother makes a happy home." I didn't display the plate. I would have, had I been able to rearrange the words. I'd prefer it to have read: "A happy mother makes a good home." Or put simply, "If mama ain't happy, ain't nobody happy."

For the most part, Louise seemed to be a happy woman in a variety of care-giving roles. The role that I'm grateful to have witnessed is the one that involved her older sister Rosie.

Louise and Rosie were part of a Polish-Catholic family of five boys and six girls. Something occurred in Rosie's early childhood years that left her developmentally disabled. Her mental capacity was that of a preschooler. Of the 11 children in the family, Rosie was near the middle. After both parents passed in their later years, Louise, the second-to-youngest, took on the task of keeping Rosie connected to the family. She saw to it that Rosie lived in a place that was safe and appropriate for her. Rosie's group home in Riverhead, New York, was just a few miles from Louise and most of the other siblings and their extended families. She was comfortable there, both with the other residents and with her houseparents. It was her home, and they were her second family. Each night, Rosie went to bed with a picture of her deceased parents tucked carefully and lovingly under her pillow.

Louise was Rosie's advocate in every way. Rosie loved Christmas and her birthday, and Louise was intent on making those occasions happy times for her. Every year, as June approached, Louise reminded the family, "Rosie's birthday is coming. June 14. Flag Day." She would call all of her siblings, inviting them to the birthday party that she'd host for Rosie. Louise's phone call wasn't so much an invitation to attend as it was a command performance. She was firm with her siblings, telling them, "Come and see Rosie for her birthday. Bring her a little gift or just give her a dollar. It doesn't matter. She'll be happy with any little thing. Just come."

Rosie once received a toy parrot for a gift. She would look that parrot straight in the eye and say, firmly, "Talk to me."

And the parrot, doing exactly what it was made to do, would say, "Talk to me," and Rosie would laugh.

In the morning, Rosie would say, "Good Morning, Polly."

And the parrot would say, "Good Morning, Polly."

"No!" Rosie would holler. "Say, 'Good morning, Rosie.'"

And the parrot would say, "No! Say, 'Good morning, Rosie.'"

Then, Rosie would laugh, content.

Rosie didn't live by schedules or time limitations, but she did love owning and wearing a watch. She might have owned as many watches in her lifetime as we own toothbrushes. I didn't understand why my mother-in-law kept buying watches for her: Rosie always lost or broke them. Louise would just always buy her another.

At the time, I saw it as frivolous. Now, I realize what a compassionate gesture Louise's watch-buying was.

Another party Louise hosted for Rosie was a backyard pool party. This one was for the residents of Rosie's home and her houseparents—about a dozen people. Louise would prepare a big buffet of summer food that always included an array of salads, such as her homemade cole slaw. My father-in-law, Ed, would proudly show off his flower garden of peonies, gladiolas, and other colorful plants in full bloom around the pool.

Initially, I had a hard time with this occasion. I didn't put the effort into seeing the souls that were beneath the misshapen facial features, awkward shuffled walks, and grunts of inaudible words. Conversely, my mother-in-law's easy way with her guests impressed me.

Recently, I heard a sermon written by Unitarian-Universalist Minister Jean Rowe that summed up my feelings at those gatherings. "When we see others as different and strange, we aren't sure how to be with them, how to act, what to say. In our confusion, we end up avoiding them."

I even had trouble being with Rosie's houseparents, not because they were different from me physically or in any overt way, but because of the way they lived out their compassion. I was in awe of them. They seemed so good, beyond how I could imagine being. And, like my mother-in-law, they were so natural at what they were doing.

Despite all her watches, Rosie didn't seem to have a sense of time, that is, until her last days. When she was in her late 70s, Rosie fell seriously ill. Louise was away when Rosie's prognosis turned grim, but family members and her devoted houseparents stayed at her hospital bedside. Rosie had been unresponsive for days.

Then, Louise returned.

Briefly, one last time, Rosie opened her eyes and smiled. In some way, perhaps, she did have a sense of time.

Thanks in large part to her younger sister Louise, Rosie lived a life of laughter, acceptance, and love. Reverend Lauralyn Bellamy wrote, "If you have known love, give some back to a bruised and hurting world." It seems like a fair exchange. In Rosie's world, Louise appeared to do that, naturally.

Louise enjoyed preparing and sharing food. One of her specialties was banana cake. She used that recipe when she made a wedding cake for me and Tom. Louise's daughter, Kathy, uses her jam recipe. Our son, Jeremy, makes the bread-and-butter pickles that his grandmother had made.

Since Louise's passing, I have become a grandmother—a happy grandmother—and I think of Louise whenever I pull out my old wooden rolling pin. I love the feel of it. So far, pastry dough hasn't touched it. Granddaughter Madison and I have used it, experiencing the joy of rolling out fresh batches of homemade play dough. One of these days, I'll make a pie crust. I feel it coming.

If Louise and Rosie look for each other on The Other Side, it's likely that Louise has only to listen for a voice singing "He's Got the Whole World in His Hands" loud and strong. It's Rosie's favorite. And Rosie probably will find Louise hosting a compassion party, serving her guests generous portions of worth and dignity. She'll likely have goody bags for everyone containing gifts that are totally useless in the afterlife, like a watch. But she'll give them anyway, just to make her guests feel good.

March 2012

Louise, Rosie, and me

"Never believe for a second that you're weak,
within all of us we have a reserve of inner hidden strength."
—Victoria Addino

Lizzy

It was fall, and, in New York, things were dying. Maybe you prefer to think that they're in a changed state: resting until spring. What we know is, things change.

I sat on a Southwest Airlines flight from Fort Meyers, Florida, to Islip, New York. It was October 2002. My younger sister, Liz, sat on my right; my mother, on my left. I treated myself to a glass of wine because I could finally relax. A long ordeal was coming to a close, and it was my birthday.

In late August, doctors diagnosed Liz with a malignant tumor on her spine. That same weekend, other doctors diagnosed my mother with Alzheimer's disease. Liz and Mom lived just a few miles apart, in Lehigh Acres, Florida. But after her back surgery, my siblings and I moved Liz into my mother's condo to facilitate caregiving. The three of us had spent seven intense weeks together. Now I was bringing them home with me to New York.

I tried to explain the wine to my mother: "It's my birthday, Mom. I'm 55 today."

"It's my birthday?" she responded.

I smiled, but only outwardly. I took a deep breath that was part sigh and sipped the wine. My husband, Tom; sister, Anne; and her husband, Mike, would meet us at the airport in Islip. They came equipped with a wheelchair for Liz and a walker for Mom. I had checked nine pieces of baggage, the maximum allowed free for three travelers. I color-coded the boxes and suitcases with ribbons. Some would come home with me. Some, with Anne. Others, we would set aside for now.

Mom would move into an assisted living facility soon. But in a week and a half, Anne and I would drive Liz to her first cancer treatment at Memorial Sloane-Kettering in Manhattan. The appointment was set for October 31, Halloween.

Some believe that Halloween is a time when the veil between this world and The Other World is thin, allowing spirits to pass through. Knowing some of my deceased relatives, if they wanted to visit this world they would find a way—thin veil or thick. I think of my deceased loved ones every day. But on Halloween, it's different with Liz.

October 31 fell on a Thursday that year. Anne, Liz, and I would have to navigate heavy morning traffic on the Long Island Expressway to Sloane-Kettering. Neither Anne nor I have a great sense of direction, but getting to the hospital went rather smoothly. We even managed small talk as we found our way through congested, unfamiliar streets. The small talk kept the stress level down, the stress related to the purpose of our appointment.

The hospital has its own parking facility, which helped. Once inside, we made some stops for paperwork of various kinds. Then, we went to the waiting room, where we would have nothing to do finally but sit, wait, and just be there with Liz.

The waiting room was small enough to be warm and big enough for about a dozen patients and some medical equipment. People sat on cushioned chairs that faced each other along two opposite walls. The chairs were attached, seating people very close to each other. Anne and I sat like bookends on each side of Liz.

Some of the patients were attached to IVs. Others just sat, their faces expressionless. We watched as a pleasant nurse tended to each patient in a kind, gentle manner. Then, she approached Liz. Liz had surgery on her spine in early September and had to wear a brace over her clothing. The heavy, white plastic brace covered Liz's torso. Today, she wore it over an off-white sweatshirt.

The nurse approached pleasantly, her clipboard in hand. We gave her our full attention. This was serious, so, of course, we were ready to listen carefully. The nurse noticed Liz's brace—it was impossible to miss. It provided the support that her spine needed and indicated a serious problem. If anything, the brace usually drew looks of compassion from others.

We were all rather startled when the lovely, gentle nurse looked at Liz, and, noticing her torso, said with a laugh, "Oh, that's great."

Her expression changed abruptly when she realized that Liz was not, in fact, wearing a Halloween costume. The nurse quickly covered up her embarrassment and continued in a professional manner. Anne and I looked at Liz's torso and saw it for ourselves: The brace made it absolutely look as if Liz were wearing a skeleton costume. Once the nurse turned away, the three of us laughed. We desperately wanted to exercise some control, considering where we were, and we certainly didn't want to embarrass the nurse any further, but the more we tried to stop laughing, the worse we got.

Every once in a while, one of us said softly, "We have to stop. This is awful." There we were, in a waiting room where others sat solemnly, and we were laughing fitfully.

A nurse called Liz's name.

OK, we all figured, serious time now. No more laughing. But when Liz stepped into a cubicle to change into a hospital gown, Anne and I heard her laugh, and that just set us off all over again.

Every day for a year, Liz wore that brace, but it never looked quite like it did that Halloween day in the waiting room.

I was just a little over two years old when Lizzy was born in December 1949. The story that I was told goes that, when my mother came home from the hospital with Liz, I asked, "Did you bring me a baby doll?" My new sister was christened "Elizabeth Frances," but we called her "Baby Doll." Just before Liz started school, she let the family know that she didn't want to be called "Baby Doll" anymore. And so, she was "Lizzy."

When Liz and I were young, we played a game that we called "Rocking Horse." I lay on my back and pulled my knees up to my chest. Liz sat on the lower part of my legs. We'd clasp our hands and rock our bodies—one up, the other down—rocking back and forth. The game was always fun. It wasn't at all competitive. There was no winner, no loser. We just held onto each other and rocked. Rocking Horse was simple fun that always made us feel good. Like a quote that I relate to—"There are shortcuts to happiness, and dancing is one of them"—for us, at that time, the shortcut to happiness, or at least a happy feeling, was simply playing Rocking Horse.

Liz and I played with dolls, but only with friends—two sisters, Marilyn and Susan, who lived across the street. They were the ones who had the dolls. They also had great bungalows on their property that we used as our playhouses.

In our own backyard, we spent as much time on our swing set as we did playing in a small patch of dirt. We had Matchbox cars that had probably belonged to our older brothers. We spent lots of time building intricate roadways for them. On one side of the garage, where hardly anyone ever went, Liz and I found daddy longlegs spiders, although I don't think it ever crossed our minds that they were spiders. They just intrigued us. Liz and I sat on the ground, letting them crawl on us, picking them up to direct them where we wanted them to go, just amusing ourselves with them.

One day the daddy longlegs that Liz was playing with lost a leg. The next thing I knew, she had switched hers for mine, one with all of its legs. I argued with her to give me back my daddy longlegs, but she wouldn't budge. Indignantly, I went into the house and reported to my mother, "Lizzy took my daddy longlegs, and she won't give it back to me. She gave me hers with a missing leg." That was just one of our ordinary sibling fights. In later years, our fights were rather ugly and quite hurtful.

When Liz and I grew out of playing in the dirt, our days, especially our summer days, were long and active. We rode bikes for hours with a crowd of neighborhood friends. We played softball at the home that had the biggest yard, where Dennis, Frank, and Thomas—the "summer kids"—lived. The summer that I was 13 and Liz was 11, we babysat our three-year-old brother, Michael. Liz and I took turns, alternating weeks. It had been three years since our father and our oldest brother, Al, had died in a tugboat accident. Mom went to work full time. Our older sister, Anne, now married with a baby of her own, also helped with Michael's care, but that summer he was with us.

Our youngest sister, Patty, was only eight. But it was Michael who Liz and I were assigned to look after. We had a big gray carriage that we pushed him in. It was heavy and a bit awkward, but it came in handy when we wanted to get somewhere faster than he could walk. Thinking of that summer, surprisingly, I don't remember either of us ever complaining. Many years later, Liz and I decided that we were members of a very small club: "The Don't Mess with Michael Club." We made Patty and Mom members, too.

When Liz was still in grade school, she attended a school-sponsored dance contest. The prize for the lucky winner: a puppy. Before she left for the dance, Lizzy asked, "Mom, if I win the contest, can I bring the puppy home?" Whether she really considered the question or not, Mom answered, "Sure."

One of Liz's friends told me years later, "You should have seen Liz dance in that contest. She wanted that puppy so badly."

Liz came home with that puppy, an adorable collie-mix. Queenie was part of our family for many years.

I was fixing coffee one morning in Florida. By this time, Liz had permanently moved into Mom's condo in a retirement community. I was only half-awake while I fumbled to scoop coffee and measure the water. Even without the caffeine, I jolted awake and screamed. Then, I quickly let Liz know that I was OK, just startled.

"On the counter," I explained, "right by the coffeemaker, there's one of those little orange lizards." I stood back a few feet. Liz used a cane when she walked now. Moving slowly and carefully, she came into the kitchen and approached the counter. Looking down at the little lizard, she said, "Well, good morning. What are you doing here?"

This was one of the little critters that Liz had been concerned about: She brought up the issue with the community board that handled lawn maintenance, asking the committee members to assure her that whatever spray used for pest control did not put the little lizards at risk. Liz loved and had concern for all of God's creatures.

When we got off the school bus, the first house that we passed belonged to Mrs. Phurst, our piano teacher. I started taking lessons first. Liz began six months after me and was a quick student, very soon lagging only a lesson or two behind me. I think that Mrs. Phurst had something to do with deliberately keeping it that way, for the sake of my confidence.

Liz and I were in high school when the miniskirt came into style. I remember, one day, Liz stood on a chair in the kitchen so that my mother could measure the length of her skirt. I knew that if I were on that chair I would have asked, "Would this be okay?" wanting to wear my skirt really short. In contrast, Liz put her arm at her side. Tapping the tips of her fingers on her thigh, she said, "Right here. Hem it to the bottom of this finger," and she got away with it.

Each afternoon, my mother called us from work to tell us what to do to help her with dinner. She never tasked us with anything that enabled us to learn anything about cooking. Most often it was, "Peel a bunch of potatoes and get a pot of water ready."

One of us would take the message and share it with the other. But then, we'd often fall asleep in front of the TV or just forget. When we'd hear Mom's car pull into the driveway at 5:30, we'd panic, hollering, "Mom's home!"

It took just minutes for my mother to shut off the car, pick up her purse from the seat next to her, walk up the side steps into the house, hang her coat, walk through the dining room, and reach the kitchen. In that time, with our adrenaline pumping, Liz and I would have a pot of water on the stove, newspapers spread on the table to catch the skins that flew off the potatoes, and some of the potatoes even cut and ready for the pot. Mom wasn't mean, but after working all day, she expected to come home to find that we had followed her directions.

One summer, while I was in college, I worked at a diner. My boss was hardworking and always seemed too tired to say more than what was essential. One day he said, "We need more help here. Anyone know someone?"

I responded, "I have a sister."

At home, I spoke to Liz, and she was interested. So "Sister" was on the schedule. Every week, the schedule read the same: "Saturday – 7 a.m. – Rose, Phyllis, Mary Ellen, Sister."

Liz and I held another waitressing job together at a motel in the Hamptons that hosted chamber music players on weekends. Liz and I served the soup. One of us held the tureen while the other ladled soup into bowls. One of us slipped up, and a bit of soup spilled into the lap of a pleasant, middle-aged woman. She was forgiving. On a second try, it happened again. She looked dismayed. We apologized profusely, grew flustered, and made the mistake of making eye contact with one another and began laughing.

We made a shaky third try, and more soup landed on the woman. The situation had become impossible. We tried, but Liz and I couldn't cover our laughter, although we couldn't have been laughing very loud. We managed to hear the woman say, "No, thanks," as she placed her hand over her soup bowl.

I don't remember the motel asking us not to return, but I also don't remember ever working there again.

My first car was a 1958 Chevy Bel Air. It was a strong, well-built car that I had bought with my own money and loved. One day, Liz rode with me while I drove on William Floyd Parkway. Something was terribly wrong with the steering, but I didn't know what. It took all the strength that I had to keep the car on the road. I did what any thoughtful older sister would do: I asked, "Liz, you wanna drive?"

"Really?" she asked, surprised.

Liz had her permit and could drive legally with a licensed driver. I pulled over so we could switch places. Of course, in seconds, Liz voiced her frustration with the steering.

"I know," I said. "It's hard."

We devised a plan: Liz would stay in the driver's seat. She was left-handed so that was her strong side and the side where we needed to put most of the effort. I would help steer from the passenger seat.

I'm not positive, but I think we stopped again before we got home and discovered the flat tire.

Liz had dark brown eyes and brown hair that she always kept stylish. She was slender, but shapely, and had a sweet smile. When Tom and I married, she stood with me as my maid of honor. Liz was always pretty, but, that day, I thought that she looked beautiful.

Within a couple of years, her look began to change. She often sat alone in a room, staring intensely and frowning somberly. Initially, it looked like Liz had severe depression. In time, she became paranoid and began hallucinating.

Doctors diagnosed Liz with paranoid schizophrenia. Her symptoms were tragically typical, including denying the diagnosis and, thus, the need for medication. Liz wandered, sometimes very far from home and family. When she had a car, she often lived in it. When she didn't, she slept in all-night diners or shelters. She endured five involuntary commitments to various hospitals. Initially, it was our older siblings— John, Anne, Bob, and Bill—who carried most of the burden of those times. As time went on, we were all involved, in one difficult way or another.

Eventually stabilized on medication, Liz moved to Florida. Starting in a new environment, she chose to use her full name: Elizabeth. She still faced daunting struggles, but she was doing OK. Liz enjoyed good friends, involvement in the community and her church, and a sense of independence.

We had a rather nice top-of-the-line electric keyboard that wasn't being used much, so, I cleared it with my kids and they all agreed: Aunt Liz should have it. On one of my visits to Florida, we packed it up securely with my flight baggage. Liz thought she might enjoy playing again.

During a phone conversation months later, I asked, "How's your piano-playing coming along?"

"Oh," she said, "I gave the piano away. I saw an ad in the paper. A church needed it."

It was always a risk to give Liz anything. She would find someone whom she felt needed something more than she did. With her mental illness, it was often impossible to know if what she said and did were part of her nature, part of the disease, or a mixture of both.

Although Liz lived at poverty level, she was always aware that others were less fortunate. She volunteered at a soup kitchen on Thanksgiving Day. And, for as long as she could drive, she helped distribute day-old bread to the needy. When the post office first issued breast cancer stamps, they cost significantly more than regular stamps. Although Liz had to stretch her Social Security disability check terribly thin, she always purchased those stamps.

Liz held strong opinions that she expressed frequently to the editor of her local newspaper. I never met the editor, but we spoke on the phone after Liz died. When I asked him the cost of an obituary notice, he said, "We don't charge, and if we did, there wouldn't be any charge for Elizabeth's."

The editor said that Liz usually hand-delivered her letters to him. He would see her coming and know that he was in for a berating over one issue or another.

"She figured I was a Democrat," the editor told me, "and she made it clear she was a Republican. We had some pretty heated discussions. I'll miss her." He and Liz disagreed strongly, but respectfully, something so often lacking between people with different views.

I loved learning about this man's role in my sister's life. He gave her his time. He validated her and her opinions. He told me his mother had been schizophrenic and that he had recognized Liz's struggle.

Only once did Liz speak to me about the disease that so radically changed how she lived. It was over a bowl of soup at her favorite greasy-spoon restaurant. How the conversation started or ended, I don't remember. I just recall that Liz looked straight at me and said, "Mary, mental illness is hell."

In early December 2006 while I was visiting with Liz in Florida, it was clear she couldn't go on living alone. An emergency room doctor spoke honestly to me about Lizzy's limited time. It didn't take much to convince her to return to New York with me.

I called the airline expecting I'd have to delay my return trip in order to get Liz a flight with me, as well as pay a penalty for changing my ticket. But I was told, "There's actually one seat left on the flight that you're booked on." I felt I, too, was being taken care of.

With a couple of days notice, Tom and our sons, Zac and Jeremy, turned our sunroom into a bedroom for Liz. Tom and Jeremy had been in the midst of renovating the sunroom, but Liz couldn't use stairs, so we needed that space. The walls were bare sheetrock; the floor, rough wood. But the sunroom had windows that filled three walls, and Tom positioned a bed for Liz so she'd have a good outside view. He set up a birdfeeder so she could watch the birds from her bed.

Tom, Zac, and Jeremy covered the unfinished floor with whatever rugs they found. Soon after Liz arrived, the sheetrock walls were barely visible, covered with countless cards that she received over the next few weeks.

Days after arriving, Liz signed on for hospice care. When the topic of a hospital bed came up, she told the hospice nurse, "Don't bring one in this house." She was fragile, but she still had her feisty personality. One day, one of the nurses called her "Liz," as the nurse had been hearing the family call her. Liz told her pleasantly, but emphatically, "You can call me 'Elizabeth.'"

Friends and relatives visited Liz, praying or just talking softly. My siblings and I were weary and tired, but Liz's care became a group effort. All of our siblings; spouses; our brother Al's widow, Eileen; nieces and nephews who lived nearby; and old friends visited and helped in one way or another. When Michael played his guitar softly for Liz, it comforted me as well.

In a short time, I spent my nights sleeping in the sunroom with Liz. She had switched to a hospital bed, without resistance, by now. I used the bed that she had given up. On December 17, her birthday, our siblings from Florida and upstate New York arrived. Mom had died two months earlier, in October, but Liz was too sick then to make the trip from Florida to New York for her services. I have no recollection of when we might have all been together before this. It might have been decades.

When our youngest sister, Patty, was helping with Liz's care, they were alone for a few hours one night. Patty remarked to Liz, "Well, Liz, it's just you and me tonight."

Liz responded softly, "And Mom."

"And Mom?"

"Mom's here, too." Liz told Patty matter-of-factly.

That's what I mean about my relatives. If they want to visit, they don't need to wait for some veil to thin out on Halloween. They just show up.

An African proverb says, "It takes a village to raise a child." In my sister's case, her devoted friends and big family were her little village. Her village tried to protect her as she lived out the nightmare of schizophrenia.

Liz had a plaque on her apartment wall that read, "Simplify." She tried. One thing that was never simple was her relationship with me and with most of our siblings. There were times when I felt that Liz despised me. Her expressions of love and appreciation for our spouses, and especially our children, came much easier. Our sister-in-law Barbara had given Liz the "Simplify" sign. Barbara was Liz's most reliable friend and trusted confidant.

I've challenged myself to remember fun times with my sister in the hopes of easing the pain of other memories. Far too often, serious illness, especially mental illness, and poverty are inseparable. I hope and pray that changes. Liz was 57 when she died in my home on Christmas morning 2006. She was poor, sick, strong-willed, and deeply compassionate.

And she was loved.

2010

Elizabeth in Florida

"Attitude is a little thing that makes a big difference."
—*Winston Churchill*

If the Bracelet Fits . . .

I had just shut off the early morning news and instantly lavished in the silence that permeated the house. My mind still needed to get the message that I wanted peace and quiet.

Although the political debate in my head was not welcome, it was still preferable over the one I was hearing on TV. Generally, what's reported is anywhere from insensitive to insane, and it feels like that's becoming the norm.

On October 30th, my husband, Tom, and I were in Washington, D.C., at the Rally to Restore Sanity led by political satirists Jon Stewart and Stephen Colbert. We were with more than 200,000 like-minded people, which was rather ironic for us. We live in Laurel, a small eastern Long Island hamlet. In the summer, we make our plans trying to avoid the weekend visitors that we think of as crowds. As we drove south on I-95, we decided against stopping at a particular rest area, observing aloud to each other, "Too many buses." But the farther south we went, too many buses and too many people became the norm at the rest areas. Finally getting into the D.C. area, we left our car at a relative's house and attempted to take the metro to the National Mall. A number of trains stopped at the Tenleytown station, but no one got off and it appeared that not another body could get on, although some younger bodies somehow, astonishingly, managed to do just that.

Eventually, we came to the realization that the accommodations weren't going to improve. We inhaled to make ourselves a bit smaller and got very cozy with complete strangers.

I admired the watch on one of the young women whose hand and mine were almost touching as we held on to a metal pole: "It's so pretty and easy to read," I said. Then I asked, "Is he okay?" referring to her husband, who seemed to be so flat against the door of the train that he could have passed for a poster.

The woman smiled and said, "Yes, thanks for asking."

Nobody was what you would call comfortable, but we were okay.

Before boarding the metro train, I had sneezed—into the bend of my arm, of course. That's what's recommended to keep from spreading our germs. A small chorus of people said, "God bless you," and I smiled and said, "Thank you." Everywhere, it was crazy-crowded, but decidedly civil.

The rally wasn't billed as a political or a religious event. I would say it was a response to a climate in our country that has grown increasingly hostile. It seems to me that the more piercing and cynical the tone, the more attention people get. Unfortunately, this is not new.

We have no shortage of topics that provoke strong responses. At rallies across the country last summer, people who were unhappy with President Barack Obama's health care plan expressed displeasure by making huge placards portraying him as Hitler. I was appalled. I hope the day never comes when I get used to such displays of ignorance and hate.

So, I squeezed into the train and hoped to be counted among those who can hear different opinions respectfully, who seek reasonable compromise that might be both heartfelt and smart. It was good to see the placard at the Rally to Restore Sanity that read, "I DON'T AGREE WITH EVERYTHING YOU DO, BUT I'M PRETTY SURE YOU'RE NOT HITLER."

I made a placard, too. And no matter how much of a hint Tom gave me about the probability that my placard would be in the way on the train or cumbersome to walk with, I wasn't about to leave it behind.

I had a different message for each side. Reminiscent of the chant from the 1960s peace rallies, one side read, "ALL WE ARE SAYING IS, GIVE CHANGE A CHANCE." On the other side, I used the words from a favorite poster that Tom and I had for many years: "THINGS TAKE TIME." In the mid-1970s, the poster hung in our winter rental on Cape Cod. Later, it was in our two-room apartment in Vermont. And, still later, we put it in our home on Long Island. The image on the poster of water cascading over boulders—and those words—continue to resonate with us.

Some people say it doesn't matter who's in office. But I disagree. From the town trustee who looks after our local waterways to the men and women in Congress who make our laws, it matters. Not long ago, I saw a news clip of President Richard Nixon talking about our need for energy independence. Nixon left office more than three decades ago, and we're still at the talking stage about energy independence.

In 1979—the year our first child, Zachary, was born—President Jimmy Carter had solar collectors installed on the White House roof. Around that same time, Tom and I started an alternative-energy business with friends Susie and Frank. Tom and Frank were science teachers at Mattituck High School and worked at the business part time. I was home with Zac, and Susie was home with Caryn, Andrew, Paul, Jessica, and Lizzie. We rented a shop on Love Lane in Mattituck where The Village Cheese Shop is now. We had toys and a crib in the back room for the babies. In the front room, we displayed some of the wood- and coal-burning stoves that we sold. Frank gave Tom the nickname "Tom Cat" because he was impressively agile when it came to navigating steep roofs while installing the solar collectors.

In 1986, President Ronald Reagan had all 32 solar panels removed from the White House. Reagan certainly had his virtues, but, unfortunately, a forward-looking energy policy for our country was not one of them. The belief was that the energy crisis of the 1970s was over. Oil was cheap, and a lack of consumer confidence in solar and wind energy made the alternative-energy business discouraging.

After a short time, we left the shop in Mattituck and worked solely from our homes for a while longer. Many promising large companies folded and some moved out of the country. Germany, which has a climate similar to the northwestern United States, became one of the leading nations in wind energy.

I wonder how different U.S. involvement in the Middle East would have been over the years if, 30 years ago, we had encouraged the growth of alternative-energy companies.

Zac—our son who slept in the back of the shop on Love Lane—has his own home now, using solar energy for electricity and geothermal energy for heat. Tom and I, too, have all our electricity provided by solar energy. The tax cuts help. It helps if the people in office respect science. It helps if they have vision. It helps if they can perceive our involvement in the Middle East without the influence of oil.

I loved being at the rally in D.C. The crowds were more than a crazy-big number. They were fun people with good, positive energy. I loved seeing the Washington Monument against the clear fall sky. Sometimes a landscape picture can be ruined when there are people in the way. But the people weren't in the way at all that day. For me, the people made the Mall in Washington and the people in America look picture perfect. There was no hate-filled name-calling or mean-spirited cynicism on display. Ah . . . so refreshing—while it lasted.

On the day of the rally, I wore a bracelet that my friend Joyce had given me for my birthday a couple of weeks earlier. Imprinted on the bracelet are the words "I MAKE A DIFFERENCE." Joyce actually gave me two bracelets—one to keep for myself and one to give away.

I offered the second bracelet to Tom, but he didn't think he'd wear it. That's OK. In lieu of the bracelet, I'll take on the task of reminding him that, indeed, he does make a difference. Tom allows others to have their opinions, and he voices his in a calm manner. He's informed and reasonable. And he goes to rallies with me.

One of the blessings in my life is that I know lots of people who could wear a bracelet that reads, "I MAKE A DIFFERENCE"—a respectful difference. And it would fit them just right.

Fall 2010

Tom and me, happy to find a bench

If there are no dogs in Heaven,
then when I die I want to go where they went."
—*Will Rogers*

A Poopsie

The phone is set to "Do Not Disturb." It's a rainy, cold last day of April. I get off my chair to double check the calendar. An unusual day: I have a stretch of hours without interruptions for appointments or other commitments. I'll write, sip hot ginger-peach tea, and have Sadie, our golden retriever, for company.

It's the kind of scene I imagined when I thought of welcoming a dog into our home again. There's always been a dog in my life, sometimes two or three at a time. Before Sadie, it had been several years since Tom and I had a dog, and she's the first pure-bred dog we've owned.

When I was a senior at Long Island University in Southampton, which is now a branch of Stony Brook University, my friend Sue and I shared a house off campus. One afternoon, our friends Duncan and Michael came by. It was out of the ordinary for them to just stop in, but their visit had a purpose: One of them held an adorable puppy.

While Sue and I pet and gushed over her, I thought, "This is so sweet of them, coming by, showing us their new puppy." And then, "We can't keep her," one of them said, "We were thinking maybe you two would take her."

I'm not sure how Sue responded, but she said something that made it clear that we two wouldn't be taking her.

I grew up with dogs but had never had one of my own. Could I take this puppy? My heart had already opened to her. I told our friends the truth: "I'd love to take her, but I don't have the money for shots and other stuff a dog needs."

Duncan took out his wallet and gave me $20. That may not sound like it would cover much in the way of pet expenses these days, but that's the equivalent of about $130 today.

I didn't know Duncan and Michael well, but I knew them to be really nice guys, and I knew Duncan was the son of New York City's Mayor Robert Wagner. All I knew about Michael's family was that their dog, a pure-bred cocker spaniel, had recently given birth to a litter of mixed-breed pups.

I pet the puppy's soft coat and, without taking my eyes off her, I asked, "What's her name?"

Duncan laughed. "We've been calling her 'Poopsie.'" That revealed some of what the guys had discovered about puppy care.

Michael and Duncan left. The puppy stayed.

"What do you think would be a good name for her?" I asked Sue.

"I think 'Poopsie' is a cute name."

I wasn't so sure, but I was often influenced easily by Sue. I continued to call the puppy "Poopsie."

Several months later, I had Poopsie with me when I visited Mona Dayton, one of my professors. Mona and I had developed a friendship. She was a middle-aged woman when she began teaching at the college. Before that, she had earned the country's Teacher of the Year award while working with children in the primary grades. Each fall, Mona drove from her home in Arizona across the country to Long Island with at least two golden retrievers. When she heard Poopsie's name, she said, "You need to give her a more dignified name."

I could have said, "Help me think of a name," but I didn't.

As Poopsie grew older, the bond between us grew stronger and deeper. An irresistible puppy, she grew to be a medium-sized dog, pretty and always well-behaved. She didn't look for a lot of attention. She just wanted to be with me. Other than housetraining, Poopsie never had any doggy-school lessons anywhere, for anything.

During the early years with Poopsie, I drove a blue Volkswagen Bug convertible. Poopsie was my traveling companion when I visited nearby friends and family, but there were also long road trips. I wasn't a grounded young woman, and I was quite fearful. In spite of that, twice I drove with just Poopsie from Long Island, New York, to Tucson, Arizona. The first time, in the summer of 1972, was to attend an education workshop at the University of Arizona.

One day, while driving through one of the western states, I stopped for gas and to have the VW's oil checked. It was a good-weather day, so I had been driving with the top down with Poopsie in the seat next to me. The gas-station attendant was an older man. He finished filling the gas tank and moved on to check the oil. Apparently, this was his first encounter with a VW Bug, and he didn't know the engine was in the back. I'd been distracted, looking at a map and hadn't noticed he was in the front of the car with the trunk hood up.

I heard him shouting. When I looked, he was frantically flinging my belongings around the trunk, hollering, "Where is it? Where is it?"

I was startled—and scared. "Where is what? What are you looking for?"

"The engine!"

The discomfort at that stop didn't end there. The attendant finished with the gas and oil. He was calm now. He looked at Poopsie and asked, "How much will ya take for the dawg?"

I hadn't seen anyone else around the gas pumps, and I didn't know if anyone was inside the small building on the site. I jolted with fear and responded to him abruptly. My fear came from the awareness that if he wanted to take Poopsie from me forcibly, he likely could. After that, I traveled with this realization: Poopsie and I were vulnerable.

Poopsie was with me for almost 14 years. Other dogs came in and out of my life. They were always good dogs, but Poopsie was the easiest, the most devoted, the one with whom I shared the strongest connection. For so long, I carried the discomfort of not giving her a name more suitable to her sweet personality.

A couple of summers ago, Tom made plans to attend an out-of-state physics workshop. It would just be our cat, Zoë, and me in our big house for three weeks. I'd been thinking about having a dog again. I imagined especially enjoying the company of a dog during the weeks Tom would be away, so I began a serious search for our next dog, looking at online adoption sites and visiting every dog shelter in the surrounding area.

I remembered Mona's well-mannered, loveable golden retrievers and decided to narrow my search to that breed, partly with our young, active grandchildren in mind. One-year-old Leah visits from Delaware. She's already perfectly comfortable with Harley, her family's Saint Bernard. Madison, who is five years old, and Shawn, who is one-and-a-half years old, live nearby and spend about 20 hours a week in our house. Madison and Shawn's house is filled with a wide variety of stuffed animal dogs.

The more Tom and I learned about golden retrievers, the more we were convinced that this breed would be the smart choice.

The adoption process for online sites was lengthy and comprehensive, as it should be. It looked doubtful that I'd have a dog before Tom left for the workshop, but I began by completing an online application form that had 149 questions. With our application accepted, we moved on to the next steps. A representative from the adoption group consulted with our veterinarian. Once we passed that part of the screening, we had a 30-minute phone interview with a volunteer from the group. She and I enjoyed conversing, so the 30-minute interview turned into an hour-long talk. The next requirement, a home visit, was pleasant, too.

While going through this process, Tom and I heard about a woman in our area who had golden retrievers. The dog people in our community—boarders, trainers, our vet—spoke highly of her as a caring person and a knowledgeable breeder. She hadn't bred in four years, but now she had a small litter and two of the pups were available.

Maybe, Tom and I thought, we'll just take a ride and see them. One doesn't easily look at a golden retriever puppy up close, hold it in your arms, feel it's warm, soft fluff, look into its brown eyes, and then walk away without an intense tug on the heart. We rationalized that if we got a seven-week-old puppy, we could socialize her to meet our family's needs. And so, in early August 2013, we brought home our little golden retriever lady, Sadie.

Tom and I have had wonderful dogs during our 40 years together. When he and I met, I had Poopsie and he had Misty. Our two dogs got along nicely from the first day they met. They moved with us to Vermont, Cape Cod, and back to Long Island. Occasionally, we took in a border, such as Trampus, a wonderful collie who belonged to my brother Michael.

Poopsie was a little older than Misty. They both lived long lives with us and both died of age-related illnesses. Poopsie went first. Later, we had Sami, and then, Daisy. It was Daisy who our kids knew best.

Our dogs challenged our family in different ways. They had to learn that the cat was not one of their stuffed toys, that destroying gloves and other items was unacceptable, and that stealing shoes from the neighbor's deck was also a no-no. All of our dogs learned what was expected of them without being enrolled in special obedience classes. This time it's different.

At 10 months old, Sadie is a graduate of two classes, maybe because Tom and I are older now and many things are different. Our kids aren't here to help. We know Sadie is smart, and maybe we're expecting more from her in a shorter time.

When I drove Poopsie around in my VW Bug, I never gave the white interior a thought. Poopsie jumped in and out whatever the weather. At this point, Tom and I probably have more towels for Sadie than I had through my early adult life for myself. When I run errands that require short car rides, I hope Sadie will soon join me like Poopsie did. I look forward to her walking eagerly to the car, sitting comfortably, and enjoying the outing.

For now, Sadie still needs her 65 pounds nudged and enticed into the car. Then, I need to position her in a way that encourages her to look straight ahead to lessen the chances of her vomiting. I was always the kid in the car with a bag placed in front of her, so I don't blame Sadie for her hesitance about rides. Giving her Benadryl has helped the physical discomfort, but short rides to run errands are often spontaneous, with no time for the Benadryl to take effect. Sadie hasn't yet had enough good times in the car to have that happy feeling when the keys get jiggled.

I haven't had an easy time letting go of regrets, although that's getting better. Holding on to regrets is not a productive way to live. For years, I regretted not giving more thought to a "dignified" name for my beloved Poopsie, but something happened recently that finally helped to heal that regret: I was heading toward the front door, inviting Sadie to join me for a ride. I said to her in an encouraging tone, "I'll make a Poopsie out of you yet." I said "a Poopsie" as if it were something more than a name.

My mother had a dear close friend, Ceil Mensch. As Ceil's last name, "mensch" is, of course, a proper noun. But "mensch" is also a common noun, a Yiddish word for someone to admire and emulate, a person of good character. Similarly, with due respect to all mensches, "Poopsie" is now, for me, not only a proper noun naming my dog, but a noun that's something of a title, a designation.

Sadie becoming a Poopsie will mean that she has reached a certain level of maturity, of comfort. It means seeing me pick up my keys and my pocketbook and knowing with just a glance that it's time for a drive together. Becoming a Poopsie means knowing that, when greeting others, tail-wagging is quite acceptable and welcomed, but you must try to hold the impulse to pee. And a Poopsie never, ever shows enthusiasm by pouncing her heavy front paws on a visitor's chest.

Sadie has all the characteristics needed to excel at being a Poopsie. She's smart, devoted, and loving. She's also a healer: I can now look at old pictures and say unapologetically, "That's Poopsie. Right there. Such a sweet Poopsie."

Poopsie and Tom shelling peas

"The earth is what we all have in common."
—*Wendell Berry*

Who Owns What?

For a couple of years, I've joined my neighbor, Chris, and her dog, Joni, for early morning walks on Aldrich Lane in Laurel, a little community east of Riverhead. Aldrich Lane, where I live, is a mile-and-a-half long. It connects Sound Avenue on its north end to Route 25 on the south end. As we walk, Chris does what she's been doing for years: She picks up litter. It doesn't stop our conversation or interfere with our pace. She moves briskly, sees litter, and either carries it or puts it in her pockets, depending on the size. Sometimes she carries a small plastic bag with her. But if not, she feels lucky to find one among the litter. "Look at this," she'll say. "The Universe is providing just what I need."

At the south end of the street is a ball field with a couple of garbage cans on its property. They're nice-looking receptacles with wood coverings and small openings for trash, not someone's weekly household garbage. Chris deposits whatever pieces of litter she's collected from the side of the street that we've walked so far: a cigarette box, a pint-size vodka bottle, an assortment of plastic and paper. She doesn't pick up everything. With regard to some litter, Chris says, "I'll save that for Greg this weekend." Greg is her husband. On weekends, they walk Joni together. Greg carries a large plastic bag and a long-handled stick with a poker at the end that enables him to pick up litter without touching it.

Every day that Chris and Greg walk, they pick up after others and leave the road better than they found it. I remember one winter morning when Chris picked up the stiff body of a dead squirrel from the middle of the road moving it off to the side. "Why let it get mutilated being hit again and again?" she explained. The road looked better without the dead squirrel on it, but, for Chris, picking up the squirrel was also about showing respect for a living creature—one of God's creatures—that once inhabited a body. It seems fitting that Chris's birthday is April 22, Earth Day.

Aldrich Lane is a pretty street. In some places, it's even scenic, especially from spring to fall. If you enter the road from the south end, it has an incline, just north of the ball field. At that point, tree branches from both sides of the road extend out, meeting in the middle, creating a canopy effect. From spring to fall, it looks like there's a leafy bridge hovering over the road. In the fall, especially, when the sun hits the crimson leaves, it's a particularly pleasant treat.

But it's so easy to hurry down this road with thoughts only of getting somewhere else. I know I sometimes need a reminder to be present. Maybe a new road sign would help. I think the title of the book from the early 1970s by Ram Dass would make a good road sign: "Be Here Now."

I'm not sure if Aldrich Lane is often chosen for a slow drive to see pretty sights. The speed limit is 40 miles per hour. It's a straight mile-and-a-half stretch that makes the road appealing as a quick cut through between the two main roads.

I grew up in Mastic at a time when we were able to use the neighborhood roads for endless hours of bike riding. It's a treat to see people on Aldrich Lane riding bicycles, pushing strollers, jogging, or walking. But those aren't common images. Like many of the roads in Southold Town, Aldrich Lane is narrow and lacks a shoulder and a sidewalk. Pedestrians, pets, and cars share what space there is. During the week, at the beginning and end of the workday, that sharing can be challenging. Cars often zip down the straight stretch of road, ignoring the speed limit.

When my husband, Tom, and I moved to this street in 1977, the speed limit wasn't posted. I inquired about that and was told, "Unmarked means 55 mph, and that's controlled by the state." I called the state highway department. I mentioned the number of houses and the total number of kids living in those houses and the number of new houses being built. I expressed my concern about the high speed limit and was told, dismissively, "Roads aren't for people." Eventually, the town was able to post 40 mph speed limit signs. Not great, but far better than 55.

Aldrich Lane used to be a truck route. Our house is located just about midway. In spite of a 400-foot setback, we always knew when a big truck was going down the road. By midway, a truck was able to gain speed, and we'd hear and feel a startling rumble that made the house shake.

About 20 years ago, an accident at the railroad bridge on Route 25 changed things. A truck driver was traveling east. Maybe he missed the sign indicating Aldrich Lane as the truck route or perhaps he miscalculated the height of his truck. The crash at the bridge caused the tragic death of two who traveled with him that day: his wife and young daughter. About six months after that, the state raised the bridge to allow taller trucks safe passage. Eventually, the truck-route signs on Aldrich Lane came down.

Tom and I keep our cars parked at the end of our long driveway, near the house. The driveway is made of course gravel, so we generally can hear any activity on it. But that wasn't the case on a full-moon night in the winter of 2012 when someone brazenly stole the GPS from my car and the EZ Pass and binoculars from Tom's. After 35 years of not locking our house during the day, or cars at any time, our habits have changed and my sense of security has been altered. If our dog, Daisy, had been with us still, she would have barked, but I suspect we would have assured her that it was just a deer or a raccoon. That's how it always was.

That creepy incident aside, Tom and I have been happy as property owners on Aldrich Lane, and I believe we're not alone in our feelings. We have some pretty impressive neighbors known for their good taste in property. For the past few years, an osprey has built a nest on top of a light pole in the ballpark. These birds that were once endangered are not only stunning to watch but intriguingly smart. The female osprey must be particularly clever. It's said she chooses a mate based on some real-estate considerations. She wants a nest of good quality, a decent size, *and* in a good location. I was surprised that she had chosen a busy location like the ballpark, but on chilly nights, heat from the light pole may offset the lack of a totally tranquil setting.

Decades ago, I expressed some concern about Aldrich Lane at a community meeting. I referred to it as "my road." Another town resident indignantly told me, "It's not *your* road." Well, it's certainly true that the road isn't mine like my house or my garden is mine. If it were my road, I'd put sidewalks or a decent shoulder on it, and I'd lower the speed limit. For the sake of children and other living things, I don't think cars need to go through any residential area faster than 30 mph.

Aldrich Lane is the street where my husband and I purchased a house, made a home, and raised our kids. Maybe I'll get to live out my life there. I think it benefits all of us when we, as residents of a neighborhood, town, state, region, or country, have a healthy sense of ownership. This is ours, we take care of it. Our parks, our beaches, our streets, even air, water, and wildlife—we take ownership and we take care of it. It's a good thing to be stewards of the landscape around us—those places near, as well as beyond our front steps.

2012

"No man who ever held the office of president would congratulate a friend on obtaining it."
—John Adams, second president of the United States

A letter to Madeline Dunham— Barack Obama's Grandmother

November 5, 2008

Dear Madeline,

I'm enormously excited about the outcome of the presidential election. Oh, I know, there are difficult times ahead. But for right now—for today, at least—I want to bask in the joy of it all.

I don't want to do anything ordinary. I don't want to be disciplined. I'm relieved that my paperwork and plans are ready for my class tonight. I can't imagine focusing on them today. I said I would help out at the church this afternoon, clearing out the thrift shop. I'll do that. We'll bag the items that haven't sold and donate them to needy people. I'll use the clearing out as a symbol: A fresh start. Out with the old. Move on. Extend a hand.

Eileen, Maureen, Teri, and Sue are among my oldest and dearest friends. Teri called last night from the Colorado hospital where she works. She said that a co-worker's husband had just informed them that Pennsylvania had been called for Barack. If we got any other news, she wanted us to leave a message on her phone.

When Ohio went for Obama, I called Maureen at her home there. And then, Sue in Oregon. Eileen called me from just a few miles away. She and I were on the phone when I saw the crowds on the TV go wild. The United States had elected Barack Obama president of the United States.

Tom was standing near me saying, "He got it. That's it. He got it." I was standing, too, my eyes on the TV, the phone on my ear.

Our daughter, Kim, called. Tom and I had wondered if she was outside with the cheering crowds in Manhattan. She was crying, laughing, and hugging her friends. She's a seminary student now. Soon, she'll be a minister. This time, her generation came through. I know some of them, and I believe that no matter what line of work they're in, many of them will, indeed, answer a call from our new president to bring about change.

I received e-mail from friends. Linda wrote, "What a night." Jane said, "There is hope." And Amy shared, "Yesterday, when I went to vote, I pulled the lever and tears welled up. I was so excited to vote, but so afraid to be hopeful. I stood there behind the curtain and said a little prayer . . . . I felt like I was at the altar . . . silly . . . but seriously."

I, too, prayed in the voting booth. I made my selections, paused, prayed, and pulled the lever.

Madeline, I would love to know more about you and your story. Your daughter—Barack's mother—brought home a black guy whom she loved, married, and had a child with. I wish your 86 years could have stretched just a little further so that you could tell us what it was really like for you. Were you so liberal and open-minded that you accepted them right from the start? Did you worry about them?

Your daughter and I were close in age, but we were two white girls with immensely different lives. I remember one day when my sister Liz and I were teenagers. We were in the kitchen with our mother, and—I don't know what she was talking about—but she used the "N" word. We'd heard her use it before, but, apparently, Lizzy and I had both reached our point of intolerance for it at the same time. We let mom know—very firmly—that she needed to stop talking like that. She responded quietly, saying, "Yeah."

Madeline, I believe you left this world on Sunday, two days before the election, so you could be free. Your ailing body kept you stuck in that 10th floor apartment.

Once you left it, you could go anywhere. Maybe you were right next to Barack last night when he stood at the podium in Chicago before thousands and thousands of cheering people. When Michelle's mother stood with Joe Biden's mother on that stage, I wish I could have seen you there, too. I know: Just because I didn't see you, doesn't mean that you weren't there. I know that. I know you'll do what you can to be one of the angels this grandson of yours is going to need. Do what you can, and thanks for what you've done already.

Let's try to keep in touch.

Respectfully,
Mary Ellen Tomaszewski

*"It's not how much we give
but how much love we put into giving."*
—*Mother Teresa*

Getting and Giving the Best

I was on the schedule at our church fellowship to teach the children's religious-education class on Mother's Day. The children ranged in age from 4 to 14 years old. I thought I would ask them two questions: What's the best gift you ever gave your Mom? And what's the best gift she ever gave you? As I prepared for the class, I pondered how I might answer the questions.

My birthday is in October. So often, my birthday gift from my mother was my winter coat. I remember how excited I was the first time I received that big box with pretty birthday wrapping. As the years went by, the excitement and anticipation of wondering what my gift might be wore off, of course. It was, instead, replaced by concern about what the coat would look like. I would have preferred picking out my own coat, but I didn't feel comfortable telling my mother that.

When I was 16, I received a special gift from my mother that I would never have expected: a birthstone ring. It's an opal that I've had on the ring finger of my right hand for almost 50 years. I've heard warnings that the opal is a delicate stone. Mine shows some signs of age, as I guess it should by now. Generally, when gardening, I wear gloves. But, otherwise, my opal has been exposed to all the activities that an active, sometimes messy, life entails.

I also have a beautiful blue glass vase that my mother gave me. I think it was for my 21st birthday. It's base broke several years ago, but I've kept it and one day will find a way to have it repaired.

As for gifts I gave my mother, I once gave her a pretty cotton throw with her appreciation for music in mind. It's designed with the image of an angel playing a harp and the words "God gave us music. Beethoven gave us God's fire. Bach gave us God's word. Mozart gave us God's laughter."

My mother was quite musical. She sang, played the violin and the piano. When I was growing up, we had an old upright piano. I enjoyed the occasional times when my mother would play. She seemed relaxed at the piano, and that relaxed me. She had a pretty voice. So, when Tom and I were planning our wedding, we asked her to sing "The Hawaiian Wedding Song" at the church. I don't really think she wanted to, but she agreed reluctantly. It was an act of love—a gift from her that was special to me then—and a cherished memory still.

I've heard that spirits like music and love *good* music. I wouldn't be surprised if my mother's spirit smiles when she sees me sitting at the piano. I think she'd like that I'm taking lessons again. I love playing and enjoy simple pieces that aren't terribly challenging or demanding of my time. I'm thankful for the lessons I had as a kid. And if, by chance, my playing makes her smile, then those lessons would turn out to be a gift to both of us.

I almost always feel challenged by gift-giving. Some people seem to have a real knack for choosing just the right gift for any occasion. For about a year when Tom and I were in our mid-20s and not yet married, we lived in Newport, Vermont, bordering Canada. We'd left our teaching jobs on Long Island partly to figure out what we wanted to do and where we wanted to be. Neither of us had any savings.

Tom got a job in Derby Line teaching math to seventh and eighth graders. His salary: $90 a week. I was substitute teaching. We lived in a two-room apartment attached to a farmhouse. Paying a little extra in our rent got us fresh milk that the farmer left at our front door in the early morning.

Driving to the nearest food market took us on winding country roads where cows grazed on the hillsides. Some grazed near enough to the roadside to establish eye contact with us as we drove by. We never tired of that ride. One day, while Tom and I talked about the beauty of the cows, one of us said to the other, "Let's not eat them anymore." We ate meatless meals for about two years. We also gave up white flour, sugar, and alcohol. It was an idyllic time in a lot of ways, but, financially, we were broke.

My mother always had a small garden. With that in mind, I came up with what I thought was a clever idea for a Mother's Day gift. I wrote a poem that went something like this:

> For Moms there's a special day in May,
> So I've been searching for a gift to send your way.
> I've looked high, and I've looked low. Finally . . .
> I found something to help your garden grow.

I put the poem in the mail to my mother for Mother's Day and, along with it, a box containing a plastic bag with fresh-from-the-farm horse manure. When the farmer handed me the shovel, she said, "So, your mom has a good sense of humor, eh?"

"Oh, yeah," I responded.

Well, I thought so. But I don't know how she felt about the gift of manure because she never mentioned it. I took her silence on the subject to be a warning. I never dared bring it up.

My mother deserved to be remembered with beautiful gifts or, at least, thoughtful gifts. I think my siblings were better at gifting our mother than I was. While my brother Bob was in his early 20s—the oldest at home at the time—he gave my mother the first dishwasher she ever had. She was overwhelmed by his generosity and thoughtfulness. I was, too.

It was many years later before I came close to ever giving her a gift that I felt was special. She was in her 70s and still driving herself from Florida to New York every summer to visit the family. She would have taken a plane, but that would have left her without her own means of transportation when she got here. She was far too independent to endure that situation for even a few weeks.

Tom saw a mid-sized car for sale by a private owner. We bought it for her to use during those summer visits. I should have known it was not a good idea: My mother was always acutely aware of every little ping she heard in any car she ever owned. I probably would have just turned the radio up. She wasn't really comfortable with the car, but she appreciated Tom's thoughtful and loving gesture.

I can't recall a special gift that I personally gave my mother. Unusual, yes. But not special. I do remember days and nights of caregiving in her later years under circumstances and conditions that often broke my heart. What kept me going was my love for her. It was that simple. My time and my love were my gifts.

I once heard about a parent who wanted to do better parenting than she had experienced herself as a child. She liked the respectful approach to disciplining that child psychiatrist Haim Ginot encouraged. She wanted to replace harsh, negative words with a more positive, gentle method of parenting, but she worried she might not have the knack. She was afraid she wouldn't be able to let go of the old phrases and attitudes from her childhood.

Ginot told her that a new way of disciplining her children would be, at first, like learning a new language. "You won't always get it right," he told her. "It will be like speaking with an accent. But for your children, it will be different. For them, it will come naturally and fluently."

I think of that when I think of my kids and their way of gifting me. I had the broken English, and they've got the fluency. They choose gifts that reflect my interests and their thoughtfulness. Our oldest, Zac, invited me to spend Mother's Day with him, his wife, Michelle, and baby, Madison, at one of my favorite places: Morton Wildlife Sanctuary near Sag Harbor. As you walk through the trail of the sanctuary, delicate little chickadees will eat from your hands. You put little seeds in your palms, hold them out, and wait. If you're lucky, you get to experience the gentleness of those small black-and-white beauties. The posture and stillness of the people on the trail resemble meditating more than trail-walking.

With a gift of garden art from our younger son, Jeremy, and his wife, Jess, they gave support to a Haitian artist. The garden art is an angel made from a 55-gallon oil barrel split open and flattened out. The artist uses chalk to sketch the design then cuts it using only a hammer and a nail. Haitians are still struggling to rebuild their beautiful country after the devastating earthquakes. When I see my garden angel, I think of the strong, resilient, resourceful people of Haiti. I hope my lovely angel reminds me to offer a prayer for them.

Our daughter, Kim—an intern minister—is a thousand miles away and broke. Maybe for Mother's Day she'll do a repeat of my birthday gift, when she made me a gift certificate redeemable for tutorial time on my computer, camera, and iPod. We picked a time when interruptions would be minimal. I wanted to be a good, attentive student, and I wanted to enjoy the time with Kim alone. She included a notebook with the gift. She knew I'd need that for referring back. Besides giving me information, she tried to talk me through my fears of destroying the few devices I own. She handled my awkwardness with patience and love.

I often wish my gift-giving to my mother had been different, but I believe that even when a life ends, the relationship can continue. I think of my mother every day. Sometimes, I just say "thank you" to her. Sometimes, I say, "Forgive me for that one, Mom." I honor her life by imitating some aspects of it. And, maybe most importantly, I keep her close to me as though she is still part of my life.

I believe she can still receive the gift of my love. It's the one valuable gift I ever gave her, and the one I value most from her.

May 2010

"Find your light. They can't love you if they can't see you."
—Bette Midler

My High School Graduation

In Sara Bloom's memoir writing class, we write without specific, assigned topics. This challenge from Sara was the exception: "Write about your high-school graduation in 250 words or less." I wrote what came to mind and was amused by the word count: exactly 250 words. Plans are underway for our 50-year reunion in July 2015.

To write about my graduation from Mercy High School in Riverhead, New York, I considered calling my friend, Teri. Among treasured friends, she's the one who remembers the details of our high-school experience.

I remember what comforted me: Relentless laughter. A uniform that concealed my deficient wardrobe. Rote prayers recited before each class.

I remember the outrageous: My friend Liz and I being sent to the principal's office senior year, suspected of wearing mascara, and the principal saying, "Get the brown business off your eyes or go home." Respectfully, we replied, "Yes, Sister," walked out the front door, got into Liz's car, and spent the afternoon on the beach.

I remember crying silently during religion class: Sr. James told us only Catholics went to heaven when they died. My father was dead and Lutheran. It pained me to tears to think of him not in heaven with my brother. By graduation day, I'd learned to separate that crap from what Jesus had taught and inspired. I decided my father was in heaven. Unknowingly, I was on the path to developing my own spiritual beliefs independent of any church's doctrine.

I remember soft-spoken, progressive Sr. Lawrence and her contagious love of literature.

I remember stopping at the convent before prom to have our dresses approved by the nuns.

I remember nothing about graduation day—not the venue, the ceremony, the events before or after. Perhaps I looked down at the graduation robe, relieved that we were all still dressed alike.

"Growing apart doesn't change the fact that for a long time we grew side by side; our roots will always be tangled. I'm glad for that."
— *Ally Condie,* Matched

Whistles and Other Warnings

I heard the train whistle this afternoon and remembered how loud it once seemed in the quiet area where I lived as a child. I grew up in a small house in Mastic on the south shore of Long Island. My parents bought it in 1955 for our big family. Our house was five blocks south of the train tracks. There were few houses to block sound, so we could hear the whistle of the train as it made its east-west run.

Where I live now, in Laurel on the north shore of Long Island, I'm about the same distance from the train tracks as we were in Mastic. The train isn't frequent. But when I get to hear the whistle of an eastbound train heading to the end of the line in Greenport, it makes me glad.

For almost 80 years, Mastic had a train station, and, in more recent times, near the station was a small luncheonette called The Shack. A summer treat was going with a couple of friends on our bicycles to The Shack.

It's been a while since I've taken a bike ride. The most recent time that I pedaled was on the back of our tandem. Being the back rider on a tandem requires relinquishing some control and maintaining trust. I can do that with my husband, Tom. Lately I've had the urge for a solo ride, going at my own pace and direction.

Riding bicycles with the neighborhood kids in Mastic is one of my fondest childhood memories. It was the rare bicycle that was equipped with anything more than a couple of fenders. Bells, mirrors, and baskets were uncommon frills. Sometimes as many as 12 of us kids would get together and bike through the neighborhood like a snake of wheels.

Occasionally someone would shout from the front, "Car!" It was a warning call sent out infrequently, as the neighborhood was sparsely populated. We pedaled along the Forge River and up the side streets, past the small houses that were summer places. We followed rhythmically whoever happened to take the lead. Sometimes we'd use the hand signals that we had all learned somewhere. I pedaled and thought of nothing in particular until we reached the hill.

The hill was fun if you and your bike could make it. It was there that I always came back from somewhere in my head to the present moment. At the bottom of the hill was a thick patch of honeysuckle. That was the hill's tradeoff. Take the challenge of speeding down, hope for enough momentum for the ride up. Or walk your bike, and take in the sweetness of the honeysuckle.

When we rode to The Shack, we had to go a few blocks north and over the railroad tracks. The Shack was a small place run by a woman and her teenage son. It was believed to be their sole means of support. It sat just behind the Mastic Railroad Station. The two buildings matched in size. But the station house with its potbelly stove was much older, built in 1882. The Shack's customers were predominantly railroad travelers. When we kids arrived at the luncheonette, we'd sit on the stools at the counter in great anticipation of a refreshing summer drink. We'd spill our coins out onto the counter from our pockets or small change purses and then painstakingly make the big decision: a root beer float, an ice cream soda, or an egg cream.

One day my friend Marilyn and I rode to The Shack. Usually, her best friend, Susan, would be with us, but this day it was just Marilyn and me. We had just biked across the tracks and were in front of the railroad station when a piercing alarm sounded. I felt a jolt of adrenalin. Marilyn was riding a few feet in front of me. Over the screeching alarm, I hollered to her as loud as I could the first thing that came to my mind: "Air raid!"

It was the late 1950s. We'd been having air-raid drills in school. "Duck and Cover," they were called. The United States and what was then the Soviet Union had a tense, sometimes scary relationship, referred to as the Cold War. The drills at school were to prepare us for a nuclear attack by the Soviets. An alarm or bells would sound, warning us to take cover. We'd squeeze under our desks, kneeling and crouching with our heads over our knees. Our arms were bent against the sides of our head, our hands cupped on top.

So when the alarm went off and I yelled, "Air raid!" Marilyn and I both knew what to do. We were on the east side of the railroad station. We quickly got off our bikes and dropped them to the ground near us. Either we thought they'd be safer laying flat or we just didn't have kickstands. We huddled on the ground against the wall of the station, in the same position we took during our school drills. I remember thinking this was our first out-of-school drill. Or it was what we'd been practicing for: an attack.

At one point, I raised my head cautiously to look around us. The seriousness of the situation was affirmed for me when I saw others reacting. Cars were pulling over on the side of the road. Some people were getting out of their cars and running. Marilyn and I kept our place against the old wooden wall of the railroad station.

And then, the reality of the situation took shape. Across the street from where we took cover was the Mastic Fire Department. Fire trucks pulled out of the fire station. Once we saw that, we realized it wasn't an air-raid drill after all. There was a fire somewhere in town. The people we saw pulling over on the side of the road and running from their cars were the volunteer firemen. Marilyn and I got off the ground, picked up our bikes, and walked them the short distance to The Shack. We counted out our change and ordered a couple of root beer floats.

I don't recall that we felt silly or embarrassed for having misjudged the reason for the alarm. I was about 10 years old; Marilyn, about 12. We were impressionable. We felt safe in our hometown, even though there were bad guys in a part of the world that we knew nothing about. We were protecting ourselves from their bombs, or at least that's what we were taught.

Around this same time, a developer named Walter T. Shirley began investing in the town adjacent to Mastic. He wanted the railroad station that had been in our town for more than 70 years moved to Shirley, the town that bore his name. Mastic citizens clamored their objections, but they lost the battle. The Shirley station was built, and the Mastic station closed.

It's been more than 50 years since Marilyn and I took cover against the outside wall of the old wooden Mastic Train Station. A lot has changed, both in my old neighborhood and in our understanding of nuclear attacks. Nobody tried to convince us that the bad guys of the world had vanished. But by the mid-1960s, the impractical, fear-inducing "Duck and Cover" program had ended. The railroad travelers had been the backbone of The Shack's business, and once the train no longer stopped in Mastic, The Shack struggled to survive. Eventually, it closed.

Historian Ken Spooner maintains an Internet site about a variety of topics, including articles about the Mastic Railroad Station. In one piece, he describes the new station in Shirley. I found his description ironic. He called it "that bomb shelter down the track to the west." I wonder if any creative thinking went into plans for saving the building at the Mastic Station. In 1959, the old structure was razed.

It's just dreamy kind of thinking, but I wonder what it would have been like if master plans had been as prevalent as they are today. I wonder about a master plan for Mastic that emphasized history and preservation. The name "William Floyd" appears prominently in a number of local places, including the school district. General Floyd, one of 56 men who signed the Declaration of Independence, was born in Mastic Beach and established a life there. Instead of haphazard building, what if developers had honored this Founding Father by urging building codes that required businesses to have a colonial look with signs that matched in color and design? Mastic may have been called "quaint."

Besides history, Mastic is a community with marinas, a river, the ocean, and a bay nearby. The strength of its civic-minded residents has kept it moving forward. I have good friends who still live in our old neighborhood. They live in picturesque homes near their extended families and have given the community the stability it needs.

Mastic has struggled with economic and social problems. What if so much of the land hadn't been sold so cheaply? Maybe there would have been fewer absentee, irresponsible landlords who didn't give a darn about the area.

Selling land cheap is one way to help a community grow. Having the vision needed to build a sustainable community is something else. Perhaps Mastic could have benefited from its own "duck and cover" program, a warning system much like we used as kids on bikes, alerting one another that a car was coming and that we needed to pay attention, just a little forewarning to help with the town's growing pains: "Developers are coming. Pay Attention. Have a plan."

I've wondered about that challenging hill we used to climb in the old neighborhood. Is it really as steep as I remember? I wonder if the honeysuckle survived the neighborhood changes. Honeysuckle grows wild in our backyard, but it's rare that I see it or enjoy its scent. With the pleasant memory of that Mastic hill in mind, Tom and I purchased a honeysuckle bush several years ago and planted it outside the kitchen window.

Tom just came in from the yard and said, "I thought I heard the 6 o'clock whistle, but I see it's only 5:30."

"Maybe it was the fire alarm," I replied.

Thankfully, it never occurred to me to duck and cover.

June 2014

The Mastic Railroad Station. On the far right, you can see a small part of The Shack.

Thanks to Ken Spooner for the use of the picture. In contacting Ken, I learned we were both in Mrs. Tribble's third-grade class. Ken, me, and about 40 other kids.

"Just to be is a blessing. Just to live is holy."
—*Rabbi Abraham Joshua Heschel*

Today, This Night, Right Now

She walked into our house early this morning wearing a baby blue cotton nightgown. I didn't know she was here. I was outside working in the garden—specifically, under the butterfly bush. For a few months now, four-year-old Madison has been permitted to walk from her back door, across her backyard, through the trellis to our front yard, by herself. She takes these independent steps while in full view of at least one watchful grownup.

When our nightgown-clad visitor gently tapped on the window, I straightened up and returned her contagious, delightful smile with one of my own. The inscription on her nightgown summed up a morning like this: "Life is Good."

The butterfly bush had been doing well growing by our small fish pond on the south side of the house, but we underestimated its growth, and, soon, it nearly covered one of the two rickety benches by the pond. This spring, we moved it to where it has room to spread its purple floral spikes. In the words of Hans Christian Andersen, "'Just living is not enough,' said the butterfly. 'One must have sunshine, freedom, and a little flower.'" Now, in a bigger space, the bush is freer.

Underneath the butterfly bush, in its new home, I hoped to find signs of a flowering vine whose identity is unknown to us. It appeared last summer dignifying the railing to the basement stairs with its floral vine. Days of heavy rain made it easy to pull out unwanted intruders from under the bush. The scent of the pulled mint was delightful.

I'm keenly aware of how good my life is at this time—meaning, today, this night, right now. And, yet, I've learned indelible lessons from personal history, family history, as well as our nation's history, that this good-life feeling can change in a second. So far, at least today, I'm not terribly worried about the future. It's the past that has been my nemesis. I've spent time and have made progress working on forgiveness toward myself and others. I recently found this quote by Paul Boese in a Chinese fortune cookie: "Forgiveness does not change the past, but it does enlarge the future."

I've also been feeling more spiritually connected lately, and although I still rant and even rage, I'm aware of feeling peaceful, contented, and joyful more frequently than ever before.

The family that Tom and I created is a source of joy for both of us, and it's growing—the family and the joy. In October 2012, Zac's wife, Michelle, gave birth to Madison's baby brother, Shawn. Mondays and Fridays are my babysitting days, 7:30 a.m. to 4:30 p.m. I'm tired at the end of those days, but I love the closeness that the time together offers, and I remember the words of Gretchen Rubin: "The days are long, but the years are short." Often, Madison sets a timer with happy anticipation of Tom coming home to us at the end of his workday. His presence seems to make little Shawn happy, too.

Six weeks after Shawn's birth, in early December, baby Leah was born to our son Jeremy and his wife, Jess. They're in Delaware, so we're separated by a five-hour drive. Our goal and theirs has been for us to see Leah at least once a month. That doesn't always happen, but between visits, we use our computers for video calls. Sometimes, when Leah's doing her sweet baby babbling pretty consistently, Jeremy will call, just so we can hear it. When we do see Leah and her parents, at our home or theirs, it means we get to sleep under the same roof together. Both Leah and Shawn are healthy, smiley-faced bundles of wonder.

The babies were still new in March when we celebrated our daughter, Kim's, marriage to her partner, Tara. We had some initial concern about Tom's father's reaction to Kim's plans. Ed, who's 88, called Kim. In a loving conversation, he told her, "My folks didn't want me to marry your Babci," which is Polish for grandmother. Ed explained, "They said she was a city girl. You know, our farm was in Calverton. But Babci was from Riverhead. Kim, you marry anyone you want."

Kim's close friend Stephanie, a Lutheran minister who studied with Kim at Union Theological Seminary, officiated at the wedding. She gave the ceremony perfect balance. It was lighthearted and, yet, sentimental. Stephanie's musician husband, Josh, played the wedding music on steel drums. And, later, the reception dance floor was never without a crowd of spirited dancers. Kim and Tara's marriage will be as vulnerable as any other marriage is in our culture.

I like what my friend, Sister Mary Beth, a Sister of Charity, expressed to me in an e-mail conversation. She said, "The key is, God is Love. A relationship of two people committed to each other's growth - respectful, joyful - this is a great blessing."

Kim and Tara are exceptionally good people. They're mature and fun to be with—all qualities as important as love. Shawn, Leah, and Tara haven't just added to the number in our family, they've caused our hearts to stretch once again, with more love and more gratitude.

Before Madison made the early morning visit in her nightgown, I'd already been feeling full in ways I'm challenged to express with words. That's what being in the garden often does to me. The colors of the flowers, the new growth, the plant that I didn't think had survived the winter, the wind chimes, the birds—goldfinches, chicadees, cardinals, and more—at the feeders and chirping from the trees, it all fills me with gratitude.

This year Tom and I have both been particularly impressed with the growth and spread of the perennials. It's been beyond our expectations and, like our family, has brought us joy that maybe only we can truly appreciate.

Tom and I have always enjoyed sharing with one another interesting things we've heard on an NPR broadcast or something we've read. And now, occasionally, we're sharing poetry. With the lilies in our garden in bloom, I recently read to him Mary Oliver's poem "The Lily" from her collection *Why I Wake Early*. When Tom read "Splitting Wood" by Billy Collins, he shared it with me, remembering his own wood-chopping days. Michelle and Zac's energy-efficient house uses solar and geothermal systems for heat. To supplement, Zac chops wood for their wood-burning stove. It probably surprised Zac to get a poetry reading from his father, but, he too, got a reading of "Splitting Wood."

For several years, we've been attracting hummingbirds with feeders outside the kitchen window. A few weeks ago, stunning Baltimore orioles showed up at the hummingbird feeder. Tom the Rigger, as my husband could be called, modified one of the feeders to better suit the beak of the oriole, which isn't nearly as long and narrow as the hummingbird's. In the early morning, we can catch the regulars at the feeder, including two sets of Baltimore orioles.

Friends and family come to mind when I'm in the garden enjoying their gifts of plants, birdfeeders, garden art, and knowledge that they've generously shared.

My life could change drastically and tragically tomorrow—or in the next moment. Time can do that. Anything can happen. No warning. No gentle tapping. Maybe the garden will be a refuge at such a time. I turn a page each day in my perpetual calendar, which is titled "The Garden Heart." In May, I read these words by Edward Payson Rod: "'Look at us,' said the violets blooming at her feet, 'all last winter we slept in the seeming death . . . but at the right time God awakened us, and here we are to comfort you.'"

Right now, at this time, on this June night, there's a supermoon aglow and there's a lily in the backyard that, as Mary Oliver writes, "closes its five walls around itself"—and life is good.

June 2013

By the garden

"I don't like that man. I must get to know him better."
—Abraham Lincoln

Blessed are the Flexible . . .

I made the mistake of looking at Facebook just before going to bed. At a time when I should have been engaged in something relaxing, I was reading the irate comments of someone I don't even know. He was clearly a fighter, and the fight he was taking on was against the people who, in his words, "were trying to redefine marriage."

Another Facebook user posted a letter written by a woman named Jane Pitt. I guess Jane's letter was newsworthy because her son is actor Brad Pitt. Jane sent a somber warning to a particular group of voters about the 2012 presidential election. She said, in part, ". . . any Christian who does not vote . . . is casting a vote for Romney's opponent, Barack Hussein Obama, . . . a liberal who supports . . . same-sex marriage."

Perhaps another reason her letter got so much attention is that her son has also spoken out on this subject, but with a dramatically different opinion. Brad Pitt and actress Angelina Jolie have been in a relationship for several years. Together, they're raising their adopted and biological children—six in all. I've heard they may be marrying soon—because their kids have been asking them to. But early on, Jolie and Pitt said they had made the decision to not marry until it was legal for everyone.

Tom and I wouldn't have considered having our kids before we were married. But we did live together for a couple of years first. One June morning while Tom visited with his mother, she invited him to join her while she picked strawberries in her backyard patch. Louise began asking questions about our relationship.

"When are you two getting married?" she asked. "Why aren't you planning a wedding?" "You could, at least, start to make plans," and "What's keeping you from marrying, anyway?"

My mother-in-law loved tradition. It's likely she would have struggled some with the idea of same-sex marriage—but not forever. If her son had six children with a woman whom he hadn't married, that,

I believe, would have been her priority issue. She tried to take care of her own backyard—literally and figuratively.

I too am a big fan of tradition—for weddings and all sorts of other occasions. I cried at the first wedding I attended way before I ever knew that crying is what happens at weddings sometimes. I was nine years old. It was my oldest brother Albie's wedding. Something just triggered my emotions, and I got quite teary.

Each spring, when I hear about the Easter Egg Roll at the White House, I think of my mother. She was on the White House lawn participating in that tradition when Calvin Coolidge was in office. Every Thanksgiving, I watch the Macy's parade and cook a turkey for four people or 14. We celebrate Christmas Eve with a gathering for extended family that's rich in tradition. On New Year's Eve, I often stay up until midnight to watch the ball drop in Times Square.

In a traditional manner, we fly the American flag from our front porch. When I became a grandmother, I chose the name "Babcia," the Polish name for "grandmother." It's tradition in my husband's family. I was happy, though, when my granddaughter gave the tradition a personal touch, calling me "Bop."

For many of us, the word "tradition" and the story of *Fiddler on the Roof* are strongly linked. I've seen the play and have watched the movie version of this story several times. Although it makes perfect sense, I wince when each of the three daughters breaks with tradition and marries who and how they choose. And I'm deeply moved by their father, Tevye, my heart going out to him as he struggles to understand and accept life's changes.

"The world is changing, Papa," his daughter Chava tells him.

"Some things do not change for us. Some things will never change," Tevye replies.

Chava goes on to tell her father of her wishes to marry the man she loves.

"Are you out of your mind?" he replies. "Don't you understand what that means, marrying outside of the faith? . . . Never talk about it again. Never mention his name again. Never see him again."

The story is set in 1905. My mother was born in 1918. She was about 70 years old before she told us the story of her birth parents: Her mother, Helen McVay, was from a Catholic family. Her father, Ernst Friedner, was Jewish. Helen was 16 years old, Ernst, 19, when

Helen became pregnant. It was a terrible stigma for a Catholic girl to be pregnant outside of marriage, but she and Ernst didn't marry.

After my mother was born, she was placed in a shopping bag and carried to Helen's older sister's home. Helen's sister, Anna, was married and childless. My mother's maternal aunt and uncle, Anna and Ed, became her adopted parents, although there's actually no official record of a legal adoption.

My mother was Anna and Ed's only child. She was raised feeling pampered and loved. Anna died when my mother was 12 years old.

My mother didn't learn the story of her birth until she was married and pregnant with her first child, my oldest brother. Her "Aunt" Helen stopped by for a visit, and, over a cup of tea, Helen told my mother the truth—that she was actually not her aunt, but her mother.

We don't know the details of the relationship between Helen and Ernst. We don't know if he even knew Helen was pregnant. Maybe he did know and, together, they chose not to marry. It's possible that one or both families objected strongly to interfaith marriage. And maybe the resistance felt too great for them to overcome. I don't know for sure, but it's more than likely religion played a part in keeping my mother and her biological parents from becoming a family.

Marriage often seems to have a way of being a sticky, controversial social issue. A few months ago, a TV news segment caught my attention. The story discussed a Supreme Court case, *Loving v. Virginia*.

"What kind of 'loving' are they talking about?" I wondered as I emptied the dishwasher. "And who's Virginia?"

"Loving," I learned, was the last name of a mixed-race couple. In 1958, Mildred Jeter and Richard Loving wanted to marry in their home state of Virginia, but interracial marriages were against the state law. They married in Washington, D.C., but continued to live in Virginia.

One night, five weeks into the marriage, a county sheriff and two deputies barged into the Lovings' bedroom, shining a flashlight in their eyes and questioning them about their relationship. Since the marriage was illegal in Virginia, Mildred and Richard were arrested. Their crime: "Cohabiting as man and wife, against the peace and dignity of the Commonwealth." The law they violated was the Racial Integrity Act.

In 1967—just 45 years ago—the state of Virginia abolished the law. The news segment that I was listening to was covering that anniversary.

Some people have strong opinions about other people's lives. The opinions on same-sex marriage I read that night on Facebook left my head swirling. I thought about the many different weddings I've been to over the years—and the marriages those weddings were meant to bless and celebrate.

I thought about the wedding where a prankster wrote on the bottom of the groom's shoes so, when he knelt down at the altar next to his bride, "HELP" was visible for all the invited guests to see. Some believe wedding guests are witnesses to a commitment meant to last a lifetime. I wonder how Jane Pitt would feel about a church full of witnesses snickering as serious vows were exchanged.

I thought about the bachelor parties that were foolishly held the night before a wedding. They often involved heavy drinking with a disregard for the special day that would follow. Grooms might be present physically but foggy-headed for their big day. What if there were a law that said, "It was not God's intention that a person with a mind made foggy by recent drunkenness enter into the holy state of marriage. A commitment made with an unclear mind does not honor the sacredness of marriage."

What if divorce were illegal? What if everyone had the legal right to marry, but once and only once? Would we hear emotional arguments about an effort to redefine marriage? Politicians, friends, and relatives would take sides on the issue:

"Preserve our marriages with the right to end them."

"'Til death do us part' as many times as we choose. It's about rights and freedom - a private matter between individuals, their multiple spouses and God."

"You people are destroying marriage as we've always known it."

Of course, catering halls, photographers, and travel-related companies that relied on weddings and more weddings would likely be among those voicing strong objection.

People wouldn't want change. Civil unions might be suggested in place of repeat marriages, but couples in love want the whole shebang of marriage.

The idea of outlawing divorce is preposterous, of course. So is a law that tries to dictate that everyone who enters into marriage does so in a way that honors its sanctity.

Was it the sacredness of marriage that was threatened when Richard and Mildred Loving were arrested in their bedroom? A judge involved in their case said, "Almighty God created the races white, black, yellow, Malay[,] and red, and he placed them on separate continents. . . . The fact that he separated the races shows that he did not intend for the races to mix."

Oh, that frightening combination: power and ignorance. Reverend Martin Luther King Jr. said, "When any society says that I cannot marry a certain person, that society has cut off a segment of my freedom."

As a Unitarian-Universalist, I seek what feeds me spiritually from a variety of traditions. One of my favorite authors, Joyce Rupp, a member of the Servite (Servants of Mary) community, wrote a prayer called "Non-judgment." This is part of it:

> Great Heart of Love,
> Help me to look with soft eyes
> upon all who are a part of my days.
> Break through the barriers
> of my scrutinizing views.
> Transform my inner landscape
> into a peaceful place of acceptance.
> Pull back my projections and criticisms.
> Replace my mean measurements
> and my biased expectations
> with an openness that allows others to be,
> without conformity to my censure.
> Restore the simple acceptance
> that was in my heart
> when I was newly birthed.
> Cleanse me of the cultural standards
> that soil my perceptions
> and keep me from being kind.

I get tired of hearing about the 1950s as simpler days and happier times. I can understand being nostalgic for those years if you were white, straight, and otherwise acceptably mainstream. But for many Americans, the 1950s were frightening times. For many, fear still exists today.

Every once in a while, I buy a card, even though I have no idea who I'll send it to. Occasionally, I reach for it when writing to a friend. But then I decide against using it. Eventually, I face the fact: I bought the card for myself. Such was the case with a card that I've had for years. It sits framed on the bathroom sink. I see it and read it frequently. It says: "Blessed are the flexible, for we shall not be bent out of shape."

Change can be unsettling. I don't know if I'd have the courage that Tevye's daughters had. Or the courage that the Lovings had. Or the courage that so many other ordinary people have today.

I've led a life that hasn't required much courage at all. I've never served in the military. When I married, it was to someone of the same race and the opposite gender. I've been rather mainstream.

I've noticed that often change is more acceptable to the young and the elderly. Youth is usually flexible by nature. And although an old, tired body might lose physical flexibility, it often gains wisdom. Sometimes that wisdom is reflected in a belief that life is just too short. Lighten up. Live and let live.

In a few months, our son, Jeremy, and his wife, Jess, will welcome their first baby. Before they married, Jeremy joined Jess in her faith, converting to the Jewish religion. In choosing a Hebrew name, he chose Aaron in honor of my mother, Anne. Perhaps, from somewhere, my grandparents—Helen and Ernst—are pleased that Jeremy's conversion and his marriage were blessed and celebrated by both families in a lovely Jewish wedding. The only shopping bag their baby girl will know will be filled with gifts from well-wishers.

As a young child, I ended each day in prayer, asking God to bless my long list of family members. Now my time of reflection is in the morning. I have a ritual to start my days, as many do. For me, on a good day, that might include meditation, prayer, and readings, whatever time allows for me to gently enter a new day. I know, too, that the closing of my days need as much regard. I'm shutting down the computer earlier and showing more discretion for the kinds of thoughts I let in.

I don't know why Jane Pitt used the President's middle name in her letter as she did. I'm guessing it has to do with his name being different from what she's used to. Perhaps that which is different makes her uncomfortable.

I don't know why the guy on Facebook was irate about same-sex marriage. Perhaps it makes him uncomfortable to stretch his image of marriage to include same-gender couples. He may need time to work out his discomfort. That's understandable, but I don't understand the anger.

It's nice when a marriage works out, but there are times when it's better, for all involved, if it ends. The average length for a marriage in the U.S. today is 11 years, with 40 to 60 percent eventually ending in divorce. Some of these failed marriages have been termed "starter marriages." They occur at any age, although usually when the couple is in their mid- to late-20s. They're childless, first marriages that end in the first five years.

My husband, Tom, was divorced. A number of other people I'm close to have been, as well. I've never heard anyone say about any divorce, "That was easy." Divorce is a difficult and painful process, and, yet, it's rather popular. Many people marry and divorce multiple times. They do that without public outcry that they're threatening the integrity, dignity, and sanctity of marriage. We're free to marry twice, three times, or more without any discussion about what God intended.

If Tom and I had chosen to marry in the Catholic Church, the church would have had to annul his first marriage. With our parents in mind, we apprehensively met with a priest as we planned our wedding. He was an unfriendly, grouchy kind of guy, and his demeanor only got worse when he heard that Tom had been married before. He growled, "Did you know this man was divorced when you became engaged to him?" When he calmed down, he informed us that, for $400, the church could annul Tom's marriage.

From the rectory, we went to my mother's house and shared with her the annoying details of our meeting. I felt sorry. Tom and I were merely uncomfortable, but to my mother, this person was an embarrassment and a poor representative of the faith that was so important to her.

Tom and I were quite happy to be married in a quaint Presbyterian church in East Moriches by Rev. Gordon Dickson, who accepted all the facts of our lives. My sister Patty enjoyed photography, so we asked her to take our wedding pictures. In a kind manner, Rev. Dickson requested that she be discreet and respectful when photographing. He asked her to keep in mind that our church wedding was considered a sacred ceremony. We were all happy to oblige. I still think of Rev. Dickson when I reach for the hand-carved wooden spatula he made us for a wedding gift.

Marriage is widely celebrated in a public way, but it's a personal commitment. No one else's commitment has anything to do with mine and vice versa. I like people, in general, and I enjoy different opinions. But there are some opinions I'm not interested in. I particularly don't care to hear from someone who claims knowledge of divine intention. They say, "God intended" or "God didn't intend" as if they know such things.

In the story that was set over a century ago, Chava told her father, "The world is changing, Papa." The world is always changing. So that card that I bought for myself, it's staying nearby. Blessed are the flexible, for we shall not be bent out of shape.

September 2012

"An hour with your grandchildren can make you feel young again.
Anything longer than that, and you start to age quickly."

—*Gene Perret*

On Becoming Bop

We're in Delaware at Jess and Jeremy's home in Wilmington. Our granddaughter, Leah, is just weeks away from turning two. From the guest room upstairs, I hear her calling me, "Bop, Bop, Bop. Bop, Bop, Bop."

In New York at home in Laurel, it's Monday, one of my babysitting days. Leah's cousin, our grandson, Shawn, turned two in October. From my kitchen, I hear him calling me, "Bop, Bop, Bop. Bop, Bop, Bop."

Tom comments, "These little ones really like saying 'Bop'".

Madison, who's now five and a half, gave me the name. When she attempted to say Babcia, Polish for grandmother, what came out was "Bop."

My mother gave me the name, Mary Ellen - with some help. I was my parents' sixth child; my father was 31, my mother 29. Their first five were four boys and one girl. The one girl, my sister, Anne, was given my mother's name. I've wondered: Did coming up with a second girl's name stump my parents?

Anne was seven, and had a best friend named Mary Ellen. "Please, please," Anne pleaded with my mother, "Name her Mary Ellen." Lucky for me, Anne felt closer to her young friend than to our family dog. Or I might have been named Pal.

I was a shy, terribly insecure young girl. When asked my name, I would often mumble it. What came out was something that sounded like Marilyn, Marion, Mary Something. I wanted to be like other girls. And I wanted a name like other girls had – names like Nancy, Linda, Susan. I knew girls by those names. I didn't know any Mary Ellens. Today I know lots of grandmothers, none called Bop, though it might be fun to meet one. But if I never do, that's fine. I no longer feel the need to be like the other girls.

For ten years, with two other teachers, Jane and Debbie, I ran a preschool: The Cat and The Fiddle Nursery School. I always enjoyed learning the names the children called their grandparents. There was one unusual year when none of the 15 children in the class had a Grandma or a Grandpa. They called their grandmothers names like: Nana, Nani, Oma, Abuerta, Nonna, Meema, Bubbe and Babcia. And their grandfathers: Opa, Pop, Pop-Pop, Popi, Nonno, Abuerto, Zeyde and Dziadzie. There were also grandparents who were called by their first names. Still others had names made up by the first grandchild that stuck, as in my case.

After marrying Tom, I added his long last name, Tomaszewski, to my long first name, Mary Ellen. One day while doing a rather boring task, I drifted in thought, and I came upon a realization. There are as many syllables in my name as in the phrase that begins Lincoln's Gettysburg Address: 'Four score and seven years ago.' Mary Ellen Tomaszewski. Eight syllables, both. That may partly explain why the name Bop appeals to me.

When I first became "Bop," occasionally I was a little tentative about it. "Is it silly?" I wondered. I didn't want to take on a name that I hesitated to say loud and proud. I remember a quote by author, Og Mandino, that resonates with me: "I am not a human being, I am a human becoming." I decided while on the journey of becoming, I would add a side trip to become Bop. I'd get comfortable with the name, and embrace it.

Of course, hearing Madison speak the name helped win my affection for it. And now what joy it is to hear the sweet voices of the two year olds, Shawn and Leah, as they put sounds together to form words, one being "Bop." I'm convinced Bop must be an easy, and perhaps, fun sound for their little mouths to form. It's amusing that both of them seem to enjoy saying it repetitively. I don't want to over-analyze it. What I know is that I love hearing them speak it.

In the 1860's Lincoln, the great orator that he was, touched the hearts of many with his stirring words. Here in 2014, our vocabulary-developing 2 year-olds, Shawn and Leah, touch the heart of this grandmother with a one-syllable word: "Bop."

Nov.2014

"'What day is it?' asked Pooh.
'It's today,' squeaked Piglet.
'My favorite day,' said Pooh."
—*A.A. Milne,* Winnie the Pooh

Watch Out, Listen Up, and Be Grateful

Watch Out

The last time Tom and I flew together, we traveled to Italy for our 25th wedding anniversary. That was 12 years ago. I've flown to Oregon for week-long visits with my friend Sue. Tom has been to Germany for a week of physics work. But when it comes to vacationing together, it's usually a road trip and, often, without much advance planning.

Tom's school is closed for a week in February, but that's our least favorite month for travel. Lots of other schools are closed then, too, so airports fill with young families with small, active kids heading south to places like Disney World. And in February, there's always the chance of a snowstorm messing up travel plans. So, we've never had a yearning to travel in February.

During the December break, we've been happy to be home for holiday events, and, in the summer, home on Eastern Long Island is a pretty nice place. So, when we've planned trips, they were generally during Tom's break in April.

Early this year, my younger sister Patty mentioned that we'd never been to her house in Apollo Beach, Florida. Her husband, Joe, has been dealing with a serious health issue, and we thought maybe a visit would distract him a little from his medical challenges. It was February, but we decided to deal with the crowds and take our chances on the weather. We would spend a week at a timeshare condo in Clermont—a convenient distance for seeing family, a couple of friends, and even Epcot.

When we were planning our week, we talked about the possibility of a day at Epcot. Tom remembered a couple of unused tickets he'd stashed away in our home safe and figured that we might as well bring them along to see if they'd be worth anything. One was from 2001; the other, 1979. Tom spoke to the person at the ticket box, noting the age of our tickets. Without any hassle, they were accepted for our entry into Epcot. A big savings—and a lesson in knowing where things are when you might want them again, 33 years later.

Patty works in the office of her church parish. She and Joe have become close friends with her boss, John McEvoy, the parish priest. In spite of the close friendship, Patty and Joe always call him "Father John," never simply "John."

I've never had a good relationship with a priest. With nuns, yes—I value those friendships. It doesn't bother me at all to use the title "Sister." On the other hand, I'm not so comfortable with the title "Father." I had a strong feeling we'd be spending some time with Patty's priest-friend, so I wanted to work through my feelings in order to be respectful and gracious.

I turned to my friends, Joyce and Vicky, two women who are smart, open-minded, deeply spiritual, and devout Catholics. We exchange books, share political views, and discuss other matters common in women friendships. We laugh together about the latest Jon Stewart and Steven Colbert shows, and we find it interesting and entertaining that, as outlandish as Colbert is, a frequent guest on his show is a Jesuit: Father Jim Martin.

It doesn't bother me to give Jim Martin his title of "Father." I feel as though I know him, and I respect him. He's the kind of Catholic religious leader that has some spine. He says gun control is a religious, pro-life issue. He's not afraid to respond to media personality and right-wing extremist, Glenn Beck, who slings outrageous attacks at President Obama, Michelle Obama, Liberation Theology, the term "social justice," and more. In an article on *The Huffington Post*, Jim Martin said, in part:

> *[Jesus] worked as what many scholars now say was not simply a carpenter, but what could be called a day laborer; . . . he advocated tirelessly for the poor. . . . Why is this so hard for modern-day*

Christians to see? Liberation theology is not Marxism disguised as religion. It is Christianity presented in all its disturbing fullness.

One of my favorite books, *Tattoos on the Heart,* was written by Gregory Boyle, another Jesuit priest. I can say, unequivocally, that I am in awe of this exceptional human being and the work he does with those marginalized in our society. Martin and Boyle are not just highly educated, progressive thinkers. They live deeply compassionate lives. I don't attach them at all to the Catholicism that prefers to keep women powerless in the church or to other negative aspects of faith.

Which of my priest images would I meet at Patty's?

I pondered and wondered aloud to my friends, "Will I gag when I try to call my sister's friend 'Father'?"

I didn't really think I'd gag. Maybe just stammer. Basically, as words go, I like the word "father." But as a title, it feels like it's suitable for one who has a higher rank than the rest of us—and I wasn't so sure it would flow casually out of me.

One of my friends suggested I call him "Pastor." But that didn't sound right. I considered "Padre." Patty had told me that John McEvoy communicates in Spanish (with his Irish brogue) to his many Hispanic congregants.

"Yeah," I thought. "Maybe 'Padre.'"

As I suspected, Patty, Joe, Tom, and I spent a good amount of time with John McEvoy. We arrived in Florida late on a Sunday, and, by Monday afternoon, we were having coffee at his home and watching manatees play in the creek behind his house. Later, he joined us for dinner at Patty and Joe's.

I'm happy to say, my trepidations vanished as we shared good food, friendly conversation, and a lot of laughs. We found Father John to be a humble, deeply caring man and a guy who was fun to be with. When addressing him, I didn't even notice when the word "Father" was coming out of my mouth. It was like Southern guys with two first names: Jim Bob. Billy Joe. Father John.

Our first full day in Florida had come to a relaxing end, and Tom and I looked forward to getting back to the condo. As we left, Patty said, "Be careful on I-4."

We often comment in a similar way when visitors leave our home. "Watch out here on Aldrich Lane" or "Be careful on Sound

Avenue." Both roads have frequent deer crossings. They've caused many accidents—sadly, some fatal. My sister's words of caution had to do with what she called "the crazy drivers."

Before we reached the interstate, we were on a dark, four-lane road with little traffic. We could see the headlights of a few cars on the other side of the median, traveling opposite us. And we could see the tail lights of a few cars ahead of us. Nothing ominous.

Then came the loud crash and the impact on the right front side of the car. Had we been in a mountainous area, I would have suspected a piece of boulder let loose. The force of the impact pushed us into the next lane, which was free of any cars, fortunately, and then onto the median, where we came to a stop. It was then that we saw the small black car that had hit us.

The car had sped off the ramp and across lanes. It hit the front of our rental car with its side. The first time we saw the car was when it came to a stop on the median in front of us. Neither Tom nor I were hurt. Shaken, but unhurt. The young, arrogant driver of the other car was fine, too. He lamented messing up his new car, which he'd bought only two days earlier.

Hours later, with police reports completed, we were back on the road. We drove cautiously onto I-4, feeling tired and tense and staying extra vigilant.

My Aunt Helen, who's 95, was another reason it seemed like a good idea to go to Florida. My mother's stepsister, she's a kind woman who loves hearing from and seeing family. We made plans to take the three-and-a-half hour drive to Palm Bay, where Aunt Helen lives in an assisted-living home.

Joe wasn't up for the long drive, but Patty and Father John joined us. I told Aunt Helen we'd have a priest with us, trying to be somewhat nonchalant about it, so as not to scare her. She's been a rather old-fashioned woman in her professional, social, and religious life. She had worked in the business world and never married or had children. Her life centered around her mother and her church.

I remember she and my grandmother visited us when I was a teenager. She usually didn't say much, but as I was getting ready to go out with friends, she asked, "Are you going out stepping?" I often had to pause a bit to decipher the meaning of her words. After a short pause, I realized she meant "dancing."

Bringing a priest along to visit Aunt Helen could have sent an unintended foreboding message. But Father John's joining us didn't seem to faze her. Her only question about him was, "Is he a working priest?"

The phrase brought me back to an old *Sesame Street* segment: There was a herd of cows grazing in a large grassy field. A border collie ran about, this way and that, herding the reluctant cows while a catchy tune played: "I'm a dog, I'm a working dog, I'm a hard-working dog."

Aunt Helen's query struck me as interesting. Without knowing why it mattered, I assured her that Father John was a working priest. This was his day off, but as we drove, from hour to hour, he took cell phone calls from congregants and his office staff.

Tom drove our dented rental car with Father John next to him; Patty and I shared the back seat. I told my traveling companions about Aunt Helen's question. I suggested that, with just a little tweak to the words, Father John could use the *Sesame Street* tune to introduce himself to Aunt Helen. I taught him my version: "I'm a priest. I'm a working priest. I'm a hard-working priest."

John said he wasn't very musical, so I had to repeat it a number of times. Simple as it was, he struggled. Tom helped out by singing it, too, and Patty caught on and joined us. Eventually, John got it and all four of us drove along, singing that merry little *Sesame Street* tune with the changed words.

My cousin Don and his wife, Linda, live in Florida. They've been Aunt Helen's closest relatives, tending to her various needs lovingly for years. On this day, they brought her to the restaurant where we planned to eat lunch. My sister, Anne, and her husband, Mike, were vacationing in Florida, too. When they learned of our plans, they couldn't resist taking the time for a long drive to surprise us all at the restaurant.

Jim and Betty are long-time friends who spend half their year in Florida. We were able to spend time with them during our trip, too, a big improvement over the way Betty and I usually visit: long conversations in the local supermarket aisle.

I called Aunt Helen when we returned home from Florida. She didn't show her usual sharpness with questions like, "Doesn't so-and-so have a birthday this month?" or "Was your flight back okay?" Maybe I just caught her at a bad time. She said, "I heard you came to Florida—and you didn't even stop by to visit me."

I reminded her of the time we spent together.

It brought to mind the question I once heard asked of someone who regularly visited a loved one with dementia: "Why do you visit? She doesn't remember you."

And the reply is, "Because I remember her."

Listen Up

Tom and I have been to countless weddings. One year we attended six weddings from April to October. Sometimes they're family weddings, sometimes our friends' or neighbors' kids. In April, we were invited to a destination wedding in Cancun, Mexico.

Destination weddings used to be a notch or so above eloping. Now they're quite removed from the idea of a quickly planned getaway. We didn't think that we'd attend, considering the expense of the flight and Tom's work schedule. But our son, Jeremy, was to be best man for his good friend, Jamie. We've been next-door neighbors with Jamie's family since moving into our house in 1977. Cancun had become a favorite place for his family to vacation. Of course, we wanted to attend his wedding. Although it seemed terribly impractical for us, we accepted the invitation.

On the flight down, Tom noticed that the watch he's worn for decades stopped working. We relied on mine until, oddly, it stopped working, too. That seemed to be an omen. The time we would spend in the five days that followed our arrival would be unusual in the best way we could imagine.

Jamie and Keri exchanged vows on an exquisite beach. The reception with 30 other guests was both intimate and festive. Tom and I stayed on for a few days after the wedding. We're terribly unaccustomed to so much relaxing, but we found it incredibly appealing.

During the final hours of our last day, I was alone in our room, facing the task of packing for the trip home. The weather was perfect, as it had been each day. I enjoyed having the door open between the bedroom and the small outdoor patio where a rope hammock hung. The comfort of the hammock had been a pleasant surprise. I knew I needed to resist stretching out for one more nap outdoors. I sighed and resigned myself to the fact that hearing the birds sing would have to suffice. I moved my suitcase from the closet to the bed.

I put my pocketbook next to the suitcase, moving a few items, like my passport, from one to the other. I was glad I had chosen to bring this particular pocketbook. It's lightweight and roomy enough for items I wanted to carry. It has handy pockets for small items, as well as a larger zippered pocket. I gave careful consideration as I placed items in different parts of the bag.

Then, very clearly, I heard these words: "Be careful with that pocketbook." It didn't come through like a thought. It was stronger. And different. I was so puzzled that I spoke to myself, aloud, saying, "Where'd that come from? What's that supposed to mean?" I gave it no further attention and filled my head with thoughts of being organized in my packing.

The Cancun International Airport is clean and pleasant; the people, friendly. Seeing it made me think of a conversation I heard on *Morning Joe*, a television show we tune into on weekday mornings. Our New York airports were mentioned, and one person after another added to a dismal description of torn waiting–area seats and a generally dirty appearance. As international airports, it was agreed, New York's John F. Kennedy International Airport and LaGuardia Airport make a terrible first impression for visitors to our country.

The boarding area where we sat in the Cancun airport wasn't crowded, so Tom and I had room for our carry-on bags on seats next to us. As our time to board got closer, we took turns using the restroom. I went first, and, when I returned, Tom went to the men's room. In the meantime, a woman looked for a seat near us, so I removed our carry-on bags from the seats next to me. But something didn't feel right, something was amiss. I counted the bags. We were each allowed two carry-ons, four all together. I counted three, and it hit me: My pocketbook was missing.

With Tom in the men's room, I had to do exactly what we're asked not to do in airports: I asked the woman sitting across from me to watch my bags. I ran frantically back to the women's room where I had my bag last. It wasn't hard for me to remember what stall I'd been in: It was the first one.

When I had initially gone into that stall, I hung my pocketbook on a hook to my left. It was a clean modern restroom. As I was leaving the stall, I noticed a piece of paper on the floor. As I turned to pick it up and toss it away, I had my back to the hook where my purse hung. I was glad to have noticed the paper and to be leaving the part of the restroom I used as clean as I'd found it. What I didn't realize was that I was leaving my pocketbook on the hook. I used the sink, and casually headed back to give Tom his turn and to enjoy more time to read. That's when the woman who needed a seat came along and set in motion my panic.

I ran from the restroom, having found nothing on the hook where my pocketbook had been. Tom was coming out of the men's room. I only took time to say, "My pocketbook's gone." I didn't have to tell him that meant I didn't have my boarding pass, my passport, my wallet with the cash. I didn't have the emerald necklace and earrings that his father gave me that had belonged to Tom's mother. I wanted them in the bag that would be next to me, over my shoulder, safe.

Tom quickly headed back to our other bags. I left my urgent message with one person after another—anyone in a uniform who looked even remotely official—a woman behind a desk, someone walking in the hall, and others. One followed me into the restroom to double check, then she rummaged through the bathroom garbage. Nothing.

As I scanned the surrounding area of the airport for a sign of anything, a woman wearing a headset came toward me, asking if I was looking for a pocketbook. I described it, and she said, "It's at security, where you came in." At this point, I was so dizzy that I had no clue how I got in. Aware that my plane could be boarding, I ran. When I stopped to ask another woman in uniform, "Which way to security?" she started giving me directions, then said, "follow me." We both ran.

I could see my pocketbook. It was on a counter behind two airport employees. I found enough breath to point and tell them, "That's my bag." Handing it to me, one of the men said, "Make sure everything's in it."

Everything was in it. Everything.

I thanked them and, once again, I ran.

I've wondered many times about the good person who did the right thing with my purse. Had I lost everything, they still would have been only things, some replaceable, some not, exactly. Still, just things.

So, I was at an airport in Mexico and left my pocketbook in the restroom. Sounds like a story with a predictable ending. I'm sorry to say, mostly, that's because it was Mexico—a country with a rather troublesome reputation these days. I had a few $50 bills in my wallet. Even if everything else was left in my bag, one of those bills would have been so easy to slip out of my wallet. And the jewelry.

But nothing had been taken from my pocketbook. I wondered how many hands it passed through. Did a child find it and give it to an adult, who gave it to security? To get from the restroom to security, my bag had to be carried past the area where I sat. How would I have reacted, I wondered, if I had seen someone carrying it and realized it was mine?

The words of John Steinbeck in *Travels with Charlie,* always seem to ring true: "You don't take a trip, a trip takes you."

When I talk to my sister Patty now, I can envision her and Joe in their home. Recently, I sent a note to their friend, Father John. We congratulated him on becoming a new U.S. citizen.

My watch that had stopped working en route to Cancun was fine. It only needed a battery—the first one in the 20 years that I've owned the watch. Without a change of battery or anything else, Tom's watch began working when we returned home.

I've learned some things from that warning I got as I packed my suitcase in Cancun. I've gotten useful messages before from that still, quiet place within all of us. But this one was different: I was alone in the quiet, packing—not sitting in meditation—and it was perfectly clear. I'm trying to be more attentive to hear guidance—and then to heed it. The words I heard—"Be careful with that pocketbook"—got my attention. But I didn't give them the regard they deserved.

When I first got home from Cancun, I lit a candle and said a prayer of gratitude every day for several weeks. I was overwhelmed with the good fortune of having had honest people handling the contents of my purse. My candles and prayers of gratitude went from every day to not as frequently, and now sporadically, but I'll always remember the act of kindness in that Mexican airport.

"Watch out, listen up, and be grateful" could be my personal travel tips. And, by travel, I mean each step I take, every day.

November 2012